ABOUT THE AUTHORS

Ed and Alan Shimp are probably best known for their award-winning "Profspop" channel on YouTube. The channel features the comedic father and son duo in educational videos including "The Adventures of Ed and Alan," "Good and Well Grammar," and "Cultural Moments with Ed and Alan." The pair were named among the top ten "EDU Gurus" by YouTube.

Alan is a precocious 17-year-old law student at the UCLA School of Law. He graduated of Penn State University in 2017, with a BA in history and minors in film and media studies. He is the founder and president of the Happy Valley Film Club and loves classic cinema.

Ed has an MFA in directing from DePaul University, and a BFA in acting from Penn State University. He has worked as a writer, actor, director, producer and adjunct instructor. Additionally, as the homeschooling parent of a profoundly gifted child, Ed has blogged extensively about fatherhood, homeschooling and giftedness.

Alan and Ed are obsessive film fans who spend hours debating the finer points of cinema. The generation gap only enhances the banter. While Alan thinks that Ed is stuck in the 1970's, Ed counters that Alan isn't old enough to see R-rated films without parental permission. Checkmate.

THE

FilmFan

Handbook

Volume One
Film Narrative

Alan G. Shimp
Edward Shimp

For Ginger

CONTENTS

PREFACE

Experts say that the best place to view a movie is about 2/3 of the way back in the auditorium at a 60-degree angle to the screen, but slightly off-center to improve the surround sound effect. This may be the best place to immerse yourself in the world of the film, but to understand a film completely, consider the 10,000-foot view. Being immersed in the experience is great, but you can't really appreciate the full scope of film without getting some distance from it.

This effort in writing about film appreciation began by taking an informal survey of people we met. "Why do you watch movies?" we'd asked. Without exception, the first response was, "To be entertained." When we asked what it means to be entertained, the answers got a lot sketchier, and when we asked how they might get the most entertainment out of the movie-going experience, people were at a total loss. We explore those questions and much more in our four-volume handbook.

Did you enjoy the last movie you saw? Were you entertained? It's simple enough to recall whether you liked a movie or not, but reflecting on why you liked or disliked a movie is more challenging. Most people don't stop to think about that, but the ability to be discerning improves your ability to be "entertained."

It turns out that the best way to maximize your movie-going experience is to have a greater appreciation for what it takes to create that experience. Really, it's no different than any other domain. Anyone can watch a baseball game or play a game of chess and enjoy themselves, but if you really want to get the most out of the experience, you need to gain a deeper understanding of the discipline.

However, we believe that film is more significant than those other domains. Communication is central to our existence. If you were to lose all your senses (sight, hearing, touch, etc.), you wouldn't be able to experience life; and if you couldn't comprehend and evaluate that sensory input, you would hardly be alive.

Watching a film is certainly an ersatz experience. Watching a film about Spain, for example, isn't the same as going to Spain. However, if you're unable to actually travel to Spain, you can at least get some appreciation for what that would be like. Indeed, not only can a film take you to places you haven't been, it can also take you to places that don't exist, or let you view things from a perspective you don't have. Further, the more fully you appreciate what your senses are taking in, the more fulfilling your experience will be.

Unfortunately, to cover everything there is to know about film would probably require a hundred or more volumes, but turning readers into experts isn't the intention of these books. The objective is take moviegoers beyond passive viewership, without getting bogged down in tedious technicalities.

Film appreciation is not about having an encyclopedic knowledge of film history, but about having the ability to evaluate a film based on its content and context. Accordingly, the first two volumes of our handbook will discuss "content" and the second two volumes will look at the "context."

Content is anything that exists entirely within the film itself. Any part of the film which can be observed in the frame is part of the content. It's plainly observable by the viewer, and is forever unchanging because it is fixed in its medium. Two elements combine to create the content, "narrative" and "filmmaking":

- **Narrative** comprises the elements, structure, and mythology of a film's story.
- **Filmmaking** is about the practical process of creating a film, and it includes the art and technical skills that go into constructing a film.

Context, on the other hand, is the sum of the external factors that shape the movie-going experience. Context is the circumstances in which a film is both created and viewed. While the content is immutable, the context is ever shifting and will vary from one observer to the next. Context can be subdivided into "culture" and "control."

- **Culture** influences how and why a film is made, and it's important to note that a film may take on a new significance if it is viewed under a different cultural paradigm. Social, political, economic, technological, and educational circumstances (among others) will affect both the creation and reception of a film.
- **Control** is the "business" part of show business. There are many power brokers vying to influence the content of a film and how it is seen. This volume discusses how these influencers combine efforts to regulate what you see.

We freely admit that you can miss a lot of details from the 10,000-foot view, but our hope is that these volumes will be a first step toward a more thorough investigation and appreciation of film. It's completely intentional that we avoid obscure references, and infrequently invoke the use of detailed examples in these books. While examples are referenced, it should be plain from the context why they are important. A thorough knowledge of films is not necessary to appreciate these books; it hardly makes sense to bolster an argument with references to unfamiliar examples. While there is certainly a place for well-documented academic or reference books, citing copious examples can weigh down and confound an overview.

Preface

Writing these volumes was a joyful process, as each thing we wrote about seemed more exciting than the last. At every turn, we concluded that the current subject was worthy of its own book. Like the proverbial (perhaps clichéd) kids in the candy store, we were giddy about every new way we conceived of looking at film and often found ourselves doing more talking than writing.

We hope that you will be as giddy reading these books as we were in writing them. We're certain that each new section will have you thinking about film in a new way.

- Alan & Ed

CHAPTER ONE

NARRATIVE

Making a film can be an enormously complex process, but when considered holistically, everything that goes into the making of a film adds up to a single story. The whole is greater than the sum of its parts. A film is nothing without its story. It wouldn't exist without its story. When someone asks if you've seen a certain film, they're not wondering if you've laid your eyes on a particular can of celluloid, they're wondering if you've experienced the story. Further, because moving pictures necessarily take place over time, as stories do, the film medium is well suited to storytelling.

The word "medium" is Latin for "middle," which is fitting because it's in the middle of the communication process. Film as a medium is between the storytellers and the audience.

In everyday parlance, the terms "story," "narrative," and "plot" are reasonably interchangeable. However, on closer inspection, the three terms take on distinct meanings.

Stories are discrete. They are a concept. They exist in the collective conscience. They are inwardly focused on their own world, and are not affected by a storyteller or an audience. The word, "story," is a derivative of the word, "history," and like history, stories simply exist, regardless of whether they are related or not.

For example, the story of "The Three Bears," has existed for centuries. Because most people in the Western world know the story, it resides in our collective conscious, and just because someone in some far-off land may have not heard the story, doesn't mean it doesn't exist.

Stories (like history) are always chronological. One action begets a reaction, which leads to more reactions, until finally it reaches a conclusion. Stories happen over time, and always have a beginning, a middle and an end.

However, if you had twenty people tell you the story of "The Three Bears," you would hear the same story told 20 different ways. The narration of each story would be different – they would have disparate narratives. Narrative is how the story is told. Like stories, narratives happen over time, because it takes time to tell them. They have a beginning, a middle and an end, but they are often NOT chronological. A narrative's exposition, for example, will typically relate events that happened before the start of the narrative, and the use of flashbacks and flash-forwards are also common.

Consider the case of Dracula and the hundreds of vampire movies inspired by him. Did Dracula really exist? No, however Bram Stoker's novel *Dracula* (1897) was supposedly based on Vlad the Impaler, Prince of Wallachia, who was also known as "Dracula" (Son of the

Dragon). There was never a "real" charismatic undead count that drank people's blood like a bat. However, Dracula the vampire, does reside in stories that exist in our collective conscious, and those stories have inspired the hundreds of narratives that we see on film.

Dracula (1939)

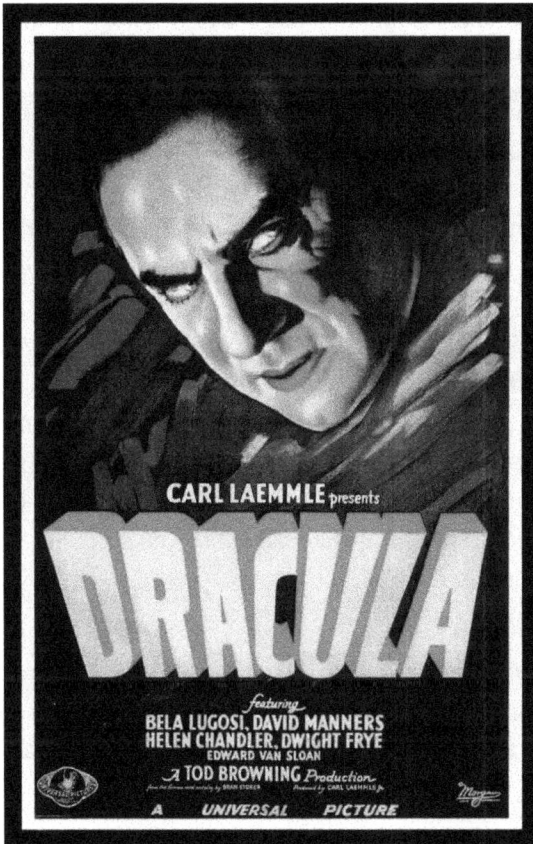

Narratives will naturally represent the bias of the narrator, and most often will be in harmony with the culture and context of the intended audience. Historians, sociologists, anthropologists, and others will often speak of narrative in terms of a collection of stories, which are chosen or disregarded as a way of confirming the beliefs of a given culture, but individual narrators will also select the elements that are most effective for their narrations.

Consider the story of "The Three Bears" again. One early version was about a horrific old crone who was cast out of her community and into the woods. She comes upon a house belonging to three male bears, one large, one medium, and one small. Having no scruples, she decides to raid the place, and fortunately the residents are out for a stroll waiting for their porridge to cool. She tries out their food, and their chairs and ultimately falls asleep in a bed. At this point the bears return to find her, and she is punished in some fashion for her bad behavior. In some narratives, she is mauled by the bears, in others she simply runs off, and in one she is brought to justice by the townsfolk, and impaled on the spire of St. Paul's Cathedral in London.

Obviously, the story took on different twists at the hands of other narrators. The old crone becomes a young girl named Goldilocks who, being lost in the woods, is tired and hungry, and sees the bear's (now Papa Bear, Mama Bear, and Baby Bear) house as a refuge of last resort.

The Three Bears (1935)

Depending on the narration, the story can take on different themes. It could be about the consequences of criminal behavior, or even unintended consequences if you suppose that Goldilocks meant no harm. It could be about stranger-danger if the narrator suggests Goldilocks' mistake was wandering off into the woods. If Goldilocks is viewed as a refugee, perhaps the bears are being xenophobic, and should be more understanding of Goldilocks' situation. It could be about coexisting with nature. If the wealthy bears are morally responsible to consider Goldilocks' dire state, it may be a justification for the redistribution of wealth. Perhaps Goldilocks' search for things that are "just right" could be about entitlement, or perhaps it's about finding a middle ground.

Now consider the possibility that the story of "Snow White and the Seven Dwarfs" is merely another retelling of "The Three Bears." Snow White is a much more sympathetic character than Goldilocks because she

5

has been cast into the woods merely because of her good looks. The bears have been turned into a group of amiable dwarfs, and presumably their stature, coupled with the notion that their remote locale has never exposed them to a woman before, mitigates any possible threat to Snow White.

Snow White and the Seven Dwarfs (1937)

"The Three Bears" and "Snow White" are neither completely similar nor wholly distinct stories. Stories exist in a conceptual Venn diagram; they may overlap in many ways while remaining generally discrete. What truly distinguishes one narrative from another is specificity. Whether the central character is a horrible old crone, a careless young girl, or a victimized beautiful woman makes a substantial difference to the narrative.

Chapter One - Narrative

Specificity is critical to a well-developed narrative. There is a misconception that generic ideas will create a more universal message. Some narrators believe that incorporating an "everyman" character or a nonspecific local will create a broader appeal. Ironically, it is specificity that creates universality in a narrative.

Imagine, for example, a love story that takes place in a small town. While that's a fine basic story concept, it isn't meaningful or inspirational. Now suppose it's the story of a nine-year-old boy named Hickory who lives in Weleetka, Oklahoma, population 987. The year is 1936 and it's the height of the dust bowl. Hickory suffers from polio, and must regularly travel 90 miles to a hospital in Tulsa for treatment. Because of his illness, he can't attend school and has only one friend, a stray dog with a broken leg that he found languishing on the side of the road. Having the utmost compassion for a dog, who like himself has a hard time walking, Hickory nurses the dog back to health and names him "Unalii," the Cherokee word for friend. Now, Unalii accompanies Hickory in the back of his grandfather's pickup truck, the dust stinging their faces, as they once again make the 90-mile trip to Tulsa. That's so much more than a simple love story that takes place in a small town.

The specificity of a narrative touches people in a way that a generic everyman story cannot. The details bring humanity to a story, and turn it into a narrative. The goal of a narrative is to express something that will resonate with an audience and pique their empathy. So even though they may never have been to Oklahoma or had a dog with a broken leg, or a pickup truck, or anything else in the narrative, they will have had some sort of experience that will allow them to appreciate the humanity in the narrative.

A plot is something entirely different from a story or a narrative. "Plot" is a Latin term meaning "a recapitulation of events." A plot is a scheme. It's the storyteller's plan. It functions as the framework on which a narrative hangs, and is made up of a series of plot points. Those points will establish the chronology of the narrative. Unlike stories and narratives, plots don't take place over time any more than an instruction manual does. It will tell you what order things are done in, but it exists all at once. It merely serves as a reference for storytellers.

A well-articulated plot is critical to filmmakers, because a single narrative is being told by many people – screenwriters, directors, producers, actors, designers, editors and so on. It is crucial that everyone working on a film be in accord with every aspect of the narrative, and the plot serves as an instruction manual for that purpose. However, plot is only one of six elements that make up a complete narrative.

It was the Greek philosopher Aristotle who first considered the elements of a narrative. In his treatise, *Poetics*, he outlines rules for narratives. He lays out six elements that combine to make a complete narrative. Those six elements are plot, character, diction (now interpreted as dialogue), thought (understood to mean

Christopher Plummer as Aristotle in *Alexander* (2004)

theme), melody (now more broadly construed as tone), and opsis (things that are seen).

Aristotle believed that plot was the most important element for a narrative, followed by character and then the other elements. In time writers began to realize that one element was not necessarily more important than another. Instead, like a great recipe, finding the best possible blend of the elements was more important.

Consider Laurence Olivier's film adaptation of William Shakespeare's *Hamlet* (1948), surely one of the best film versions of one of the greatest plays ever written. All the elements in the film combine to create a superlative piece. It would be impossible to regard the plot as more important than the characters, and clearly the dialogue in Hamlet, with its numerous celebrated quotes, is extraordinary. The great revenge theme and the mystical tone are also intrinsic to the film, and finally, the spectacle of the final fight scene, which leaves half of the cast dead, caps off an amazing work of art. Shakespeare (and Olivier) understood that successfully employing all of the elements in a balanced fashion would create the best possible narrative.

In the following chapters, we will consider each of those six elements in greater detail. By looking at these elements individually, it will become more apparent how they work together. Then we will look at commonly used narrative devices and learn how to analyze and appreciate a film using those elements and devices as a guide.

KEY POINTS:

- Because film is an artform that takes place over time, it is ideally suited for storytelling.
- The terms "story," "narrative," and "plot" are not interchangeable.
- Stories are discreet constructs that exist in the collective conscience.
- Narratives are the way in which a story is told.
- Both stories and narratives happen over time.
- While stories are always chronological, narratives rarely are.
- Narratives are always told with a bias.
- The same story can have different themes depending on the narrative.
- Specificity distinguishes one narrative from another and creates a resonance with the audience.
- A plot is a narrative's plan.
- Plots do not take place over time.
- Because filmmaking is a collaborative effort, a well-articulated plot is necessary for project management.
- In addition to plot, there are five other elements that combine to create a

narrative - character, dialogue, theme, tone, and opsis.

- No single element is more important than the others.
- All of the elements must be combined to create the perfect narrative recipe.
- An analysis of a film using the dramatic elements as a guide is a good way to critique and better appreciate a film.

CHAPTER TWO

PLOT

Aristotle believed in the supremacy of plot over the other elements. The purpose of life, he said, is established by actions. In drama, actions are what constitute plot. Therefore, plot, according to Aristotle, should be revered over all the other elements. Aristotle, one of the first people to consider things like this, was certainly an important philosopher, however many of his ideas have been discredited. While plot is an important element, it isn't necessarily more important than the other five elements of drama.

Many people subscribe to the notion that there are a limited number of plots in existence, and that each narrative employs some variation of those plots. Some place the number as low as 3 plots, and others place it as high as 33 plots. Of course, there are people who will make a claim for every number in between, which leads to the conclusion that it's a matter of opinion and perspective. There is, however, a more pragmatic approach.

Consider the paradigm of the *Rota Fortunae*, a concept most closely associated with Fortuna, the Roman goddess of fortune. The *Rota Fortunae*, or "wheel of fortune," is manipulated by the goddess, and is an allegory for the fate of mankind. A person, whose fate is fixed to the wheel, will find his fortune rising or falling according to the capricious whims of Fortuna. One of four possible things could happen as the wheel spins; fortunes could rise, remain fortunate, fall, or remain unfortunate. Such is the case with the central characters of plots. Their fortunes could rise, remain fortunate, fall, or remain unfortunate. Accordingly, it would be fair to say there only are four types of basic plots.

The concept of the wheel of fortune began with the ancient Babylonians, who, having settled in the "fertile crescent," transitioned from a hunter-gatherer society to an agrarian society. In addition to agriculture, they also developed writing, and told relatively sophisticated stories. Naturally, those stories were associated with agriculture, and served as a metaphor for life.

They noted that in the spring, tiny seeds under the soil would sprout up against all odds and blossom, and so the Babylonians told stories about characters that would prevail in a mighty struggle. The hero might have to vanquish a powerful enemy, but he would ultimately blossom, and win his true love. This is the story of the "rising" or "comic" hero.

In the summer, spring blossoms would flourish and bear fruit, and so the Babylonians created stories about characters that were already fortunate. They might be kings or queens or superheroes. Their fortune is

Rota Fortunae – The Wheel of Fortune

Philosophy Consoling Boethius and Fortune Turning the Wheel

Coëtivy Master about 1460 – 1470 J. Paul Getty Museum

15

static; it neither rises nor falls. The hero wins the day and returns again and again to defeat his enemies. This is the story of the "fortunate" or "romantic" hero.

In the fall, their plants would decline and rot, and the Babylonians spun stories about characters who see their fortunes decline and rot. These heroes are all-powerful figures at the beginning of the story, but they have character flaws, and it is their undoing. These are the "falling" or "tragic" heroes.

In the winter the ground would lie fallow, and the Babylonians concocted stories about characters whose fortune neither rose nor fell. Like most people, they are neither great nor powerful, and they never attain greatness, but suffer outrageous fortune on an ongoing basis. These are the "unfortunate" or "ironic" heroes.

Just as the seasons come and go as if on a giant rotating wheel, the fortunes of characters rise and fall in the same manner. Thus, there are four types of plots. The fortunes of the central character will either rise from low fortune to a higher fortune, remain fortunate, fall from fortunate to unfortunate, or begin in an unfortunate state and remain there.

During the narrative, a character will have both gains and setbacks. Fortunes may rise and fall somewhat within the narrative, but ultimately it is the change in fortune (or lack of change) at the end of the narrative, relative to the beginning, that dictates the type of plot.

Narratives that follow the trajectory of an ironic (unfortunate) hero or comic (rising) hero are often humorous or light-hearted. Narratives that follow the journey of a romantic (fortunate) hero or tragic (falling) hero tend to have a more serious tone. However, this is not an absolute!

For example, there are many comic-tragedies, where an audience might delight in the humor of seeing a powerful, tragic figure get what's coming to him. Take for example, *Groundhog Day* (1993). The central character is an arrogant weatherman who must relive Groundhog Day over and over again until he is humbled into doing the right thing. It's a funny movie, but it has a tragic plot line. The humor comes from his misfortune.

There are also many dramas that have a comic plotline, where a young hero is in a dramatic struggle to survive the odds against him. In *Star Wars, A New Hope* (1977) the central character begins as a simple farm boy, but after numerous struggles, he saves the galaxy. He's the hero of a comic plotline because his fortune rises, but the film is more of a dramatic adventure than a laugh-out-loud comedy.

It is important to note that the plotline is associated with the narrative and not the story. The narrative has a narrower focus than the larger story. For example, General Ulysses S. Grant was a major figure of the American Civil War and it would be reasonable to assume that any story about that war would include him. Nonetheless, the movie, *Gettysburg* (1993) focuses on the narrative of General Lee, and General Grant is not seen in the film. In fact, he was in Vicksburg, Mississippi during that battle. The plotline is associated with Lee's narrative and not the larger story of the Civil War.

It's important to understand that there are MANY ways to describe plots. Experts (as well as people who claim to be experts) have analyzed this, interpreted it, reinterpreted it, and misinterpreted it, leading to disagreements and confusion.

The ancient Roman drama critic, Horace, asserted in his *Ars Poetica* that a proper drama must have a 5-act structure – probably because the best-known playwright of the time, Seneca, preferred it. The concept was later embraced by Renaissance playwrights (such as Shakespeare), who championed anything from the classical period. However, there is no practical reason why a five-act structure should be superior to any other structure. Nonetheless, the idea then persisted unquestioned right through the 19th century.

In his 1863 book, *Technique of the Drama,* German novelist and playwright, Gustav Freytag, drew a crude diagram reflecting his understanding of the five-act structure. Freytag believed that the five acts of a story are: exposition, rising action, climax, falling action, and denouement. His drawing became known as "Freytag's pyramid," and has been passed down from generation to generation for more than 150 years. In fact, it continues to be taught in most high schools to this day, ***despite being a completely discredited depiction of plot!***

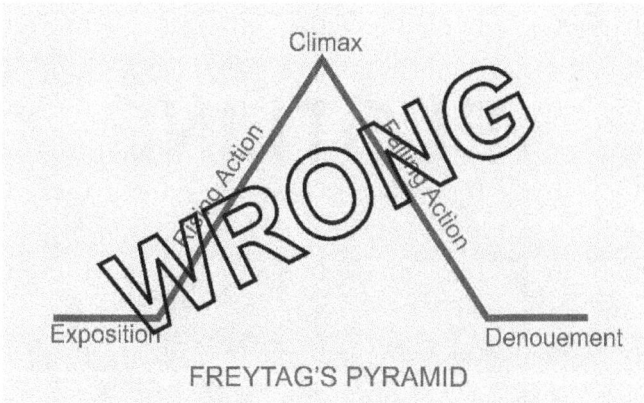

Climax

Rising Action

Falling Action

WRONG

Exposition

Denouement

FREYTAG'S PYRAMID

A plot is really a collection of "plot points," and a "plot line" is the curve that connects the points. It's just like algebra. The "X" axis is time. All narratives happen over time, even if they are not told in chronological order. The "Y" axis is tension. The farther the central character gets from the X axis over time, the more tension there is in the narrative until the end.

There are certain plot points that are common to all narratives. The very first point on the line is the "point of attack." The point of attack is the first instant in a narrative. It resides at the origin (0,0) on the graph; nothing comes before it and everything is after it. It is always the first frame of film.

The second common point on the line is the "inciting incident." It resides on the X axis but is some point in time away from the origin. The part of the plot line, that is flat across the X axis between the point of attack and the inciting incident is the "primary stasis" or

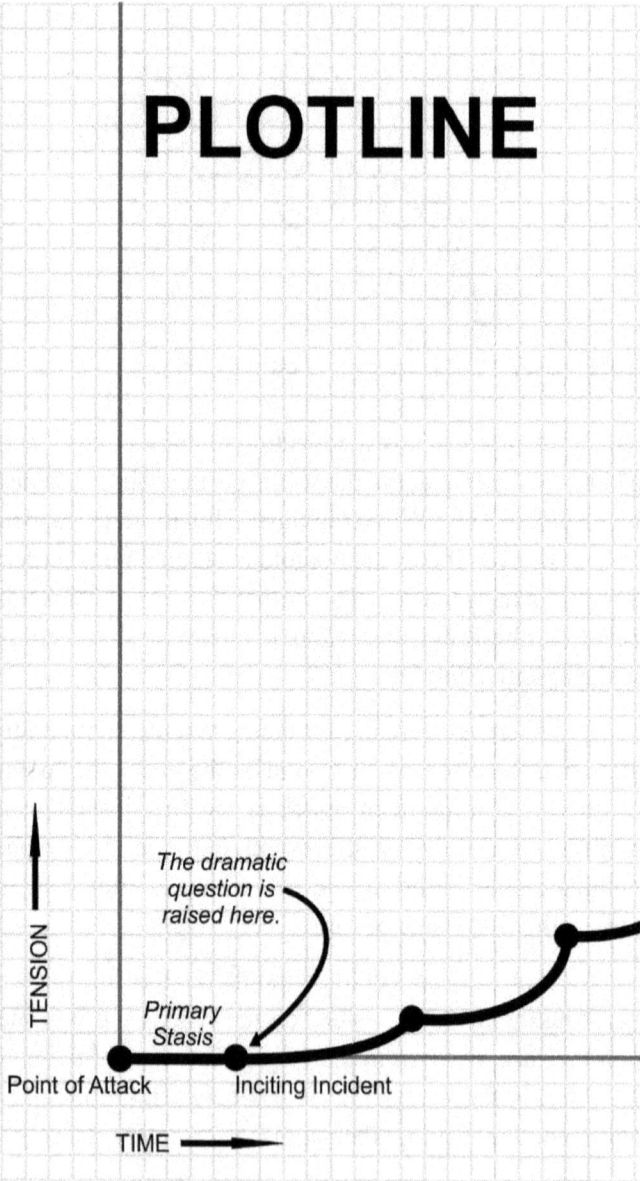

PLOTLINE

The dramatic
question is
raised here.

TENSION

Primary
Stasis

Point of Attack

Inciting Incident

TIME

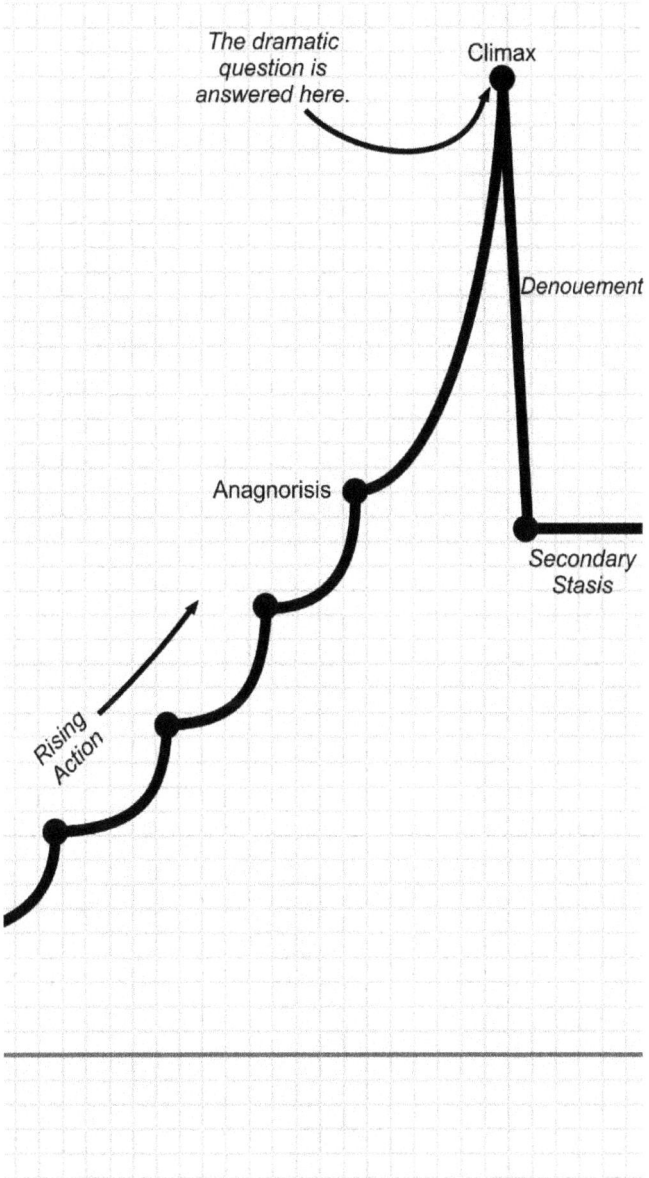

The dramatic question is answered here.

Climax

Denouement

Anagnorisis

Secondary Stasis

Rising Action

"ordinary life." In this part of the narrative the audience learns about the universe of the film. They learn how things normally run, and they learn the rules of the universe. They will also be introduced to some of the characters. Frequently this section will include an "I want" speech or song, where the central character will relate his or her desires.

The primary stasis will often include a character or element that is exogenous to the ordinary life as a mechanism to motivate exposition. This usually takes the form of "the new guy." The new guy arrives on the scene for one purpose – so that the other characters are motivated to explain to him how things ordinarily work in their universe. The new guy doesn't disrupt the ordinary life and should not be construed as truly altering the status quo. In fact, the new guy will sometimes disappear from the narrative once the bulk of the exposition has been related.

Some people will use the term "exposition" interchangeably with "stasis," but exposition can happen at any time during the narrative. As new characters and places are encountered throughout the narrative, more exposition will be revealed. However, it is important that exposition critical to the narrative be revealed as early as possible. For example, if the central character has some special ability and it is important to the resolution of the narrative, it's vital that the audience learn about it in the opening moments. If it isn't mentioned until the end, the audience will feel cheated because the universe has been altered. A classic example of this happens at the end of *The Wizard of Oz* (1939), when Glinda, the good witch, informs Dorothy that she had the power to go home all along; she only had to click the heels of her ruby slippers together three times, and say, "There's no place like home."

After the ordinary life has been described to the audience, the inciting incident will take place. Narratives are a series of actions and reactions. The inciting incident disrupts the ordinary life and sets in motion the chain of actions and reactions. The inciting incident is the part of the narrative that is associated with phrases like, " . . . then one day . . . ," " . . . all of a sudden . . ." or ". . . unexpectedly . . ."

The inciting incident will provoke the central character into action and give rise to the "dramatic question." The dramatic question is the main thing the central character (and the audience) would like to see resolved. "Who committed the crime?" "Will the hero win the girl?" "Will the central character get back home?"

At this point in the narrative, the stakes are usually minimal, and the central character may not be particularly motivated. The tension of the narrative begins, but it's minimal. Frequently the rising hero or the fortunate hero will be reluctant to act and will only do so with further provocation. The rising hero is usually intimidated at the outset because he doesn't have the skills

to succeed. The naïve young hero often dreams big but is unprepared for the journey ahead; think of Frodo leaving the shire in *The Lord of the Rings: The Fellowship of the Ring* (2001). The fortunate hero, on the other hand, has been down this path before, and is reluctant to get involved again. The wise-cracking veteran may be bored or unwilling to get involved; think of Philip Marlowe in *Marlowe* (1969).

The falling or unfortunate heroes are more likely to be overly confident and take immediate action. The falling hero is arrogant. He believes himself invincible and readily takes up the challenge, thinking he couldn't possibly fail. Think of Victor Frankenstein in *Frankenstein* (1931). The unfortunate hero is a born loser. He seizes the call to action out of desperation. He has nothing to lose. He has failed time and time again, but somehow believes that this time it will be different. Think of Navin in *The Jerk* (1979), or the great slapstick comedians, like Laurel and Hardy, The Three Stooges, or Buster Keaton.

After the inciting incident, each action begets a slightly stronger reaction in the pursuit of an answer to the dramatic question, and the tension rises. It will often pass through a point called "anagnorisis." Anagnorisis is a moment of profound discovery, but it is NOT the climax of the narrative. It is the moment when the rising or fortunate hero realizes that he just might succeed, or the falling or unfortunate hero realizes that he just might fail. It's usually a "Holy crap!" moment of realization at a "point of no return." It is at this point that the hero realizes that there is no turning back, and that the struggle must

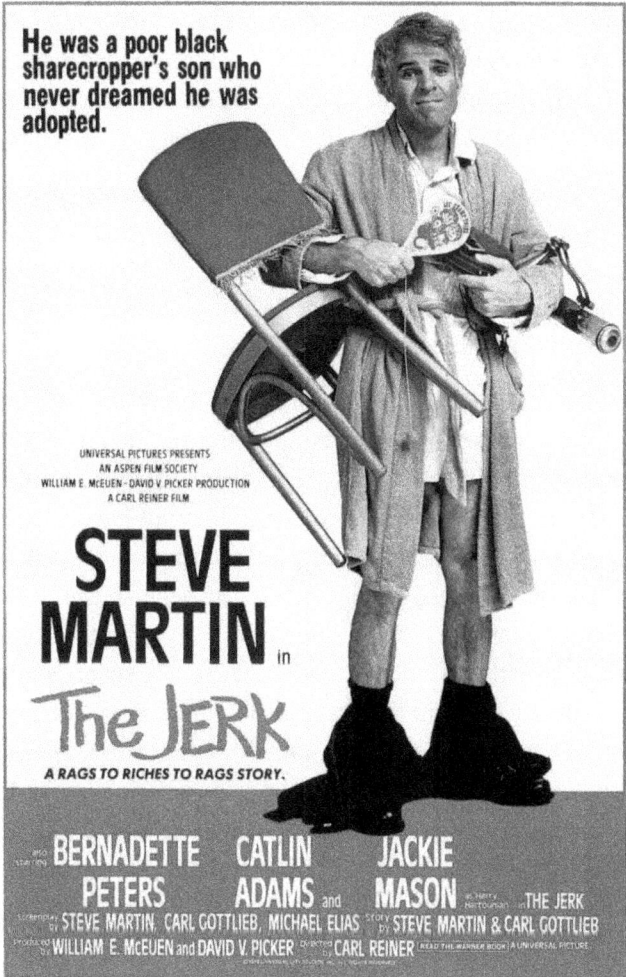

The Jerk (1979)

continue to its conclusion. For example, in *Chinatown* (1974), anagnorisis comes when private investigator J.J. "Jake" Gittes learns that Katherine is both Evelyn's sister and her daughter - a shocking revelation that impels the film to its conclusion.

Anagnorisis results in "peripeteia," an abrupt turn of events. The reluctant hero is no longer reluctant, and the confident hero has some serious doubts. It is important to remember, however, that the narrative is not over at this point; it is not the climax.

Anagnorisis is frequently followed by the "supreme ordeal" (roughly equivalent to a "final boss" in gaming), a head-to-head fight between the central character and his nemesis. While it does not have to be a physical confrontation, usually, all the support characters have been defeated or are otherwise occupied and the central character must face the antagonist alone. Sometimes it will be after a protracted chase scene, and it will often happen in the antagonist's lair, just to give him that extra edge. On the other hand, some special knowledge or experience will allow the hero to prevail. In *Star Wars Episode IV: A New Hope* (1977), after all the other pilots are defeated, and his allies are otherwise occupied, Luke abandons technology and "uses the force," to destroy the Death Star.

This leads to a climax. The climax is the moment of maximum tension. It is the instant that the battle is won or lost. There is an explosion, or the bride says, "I do," or the guilty party confesses. It is also the moment when the dramatic question is answered. Who committed the crime? – The butler did it. Will the hero win the girl? – She's all his. Will the central character get back home? – There's a hero's welcome.

The rising hero wins a prize or accomplishes something at the end of the story. In *Jaws* (1975), Chief Brody kills the shark and saves the community. The fortunate hero rides off into the sunset but will return to fight again another day. In *Superman – The Movie* (1978), the title character takes the bad guys to jail, proudly states that "no 'thanks' are necessary" and then does a victory lap around the earth. The tragic hero will not only be made aware of his shortcomings at the end of the story but must also pay a price – frequently death. In *Citizen Kane* (1941), Charles Kane realizes the limitations of money and dies lonely and misunderstood. The unfortunate hero, having lost out again, will soldier on because there's nothing else to do. In *Annie Hall* (1977), Alvy Singer realizes that meaningful relationships are elusive, but the pursuit of them brings meaning to life.

Once the climax has been reached, the narrative is nearly over. It is imperative that the climax comes at the end of the narrative, but that's not always the case. The great film director Roger Corman reportedly admonished, "When the monster is dead, the movie is over." Yes, a few loose ends may be tied up after the climax of the narrative, but if the narrative continues at length beyond the climax or continues by having even more plot twists or secondary climaxes, it can become painful. This frequently happens in a mystery, where the hero explains in detail how all the clues were put together after the bad guy has already been apprehended.

Occasionally a narrative will introduce an unexpected element or character at the climax to resolve an otherwise unresolvable mess. This is called a *deus ex machina*, a Greek term that literally means, "god from the machine." In the ancient Greek theatre (when drama was still in its infancy) plays would frequently end when an actor portraying a god would be lowered via a crane (the machine) onto the stage to resolve all the problems of the narrative via pronouncement. Of course, that's a very unsatisfying way to end a narrative, but sometimes it can be used for comic effect. In *Shaun of the Dead* (2004), the central characters are hopelessly cornered by zombies, when suddenly the army arrives to whisk them to safety and kill the zombies.

At last, narratives end with a secondary stasis. The chain of action and reaction has tempered, and the tension no longer grows over time. However, this stasis is at a higher level than the primary stasis, because having gone on the journey, things will never be the same.

It is also possible for a story will have a somewhat ambiguous ending or a cliffhanger. This is frequently done in serials or to allow room for a sequel. This is a "The End . . . or is it?" story. For example, in *The Blob* (1958), the monster is taken to the arctic where it should remain frozen forever. The words "The End" appear on the screen briefly but they quickly morph into a big "?"

Indeed there was a sequel. In *Beware! The Blob* (1972), the amorphous monster is retrieved from the frozen tundra and oozes back to life.

There is a technical distinction between a sequel and a serial. Serial films use the same characters in new adventures, but those films are discreet and don't need to be watched in a particular order. Serials most often involve fortunate heroes such as the Sherlock Holmes, Charlie Chan, or The Lone Ranger serials, or unfortunate heroes such as the Blondie, Our Gang, or Francis the Talking Mule serials.

A sequel, on the other hand, will pick up the story from the end of the previous film, (the secondary stasis). Often a rising hero in the first film will become a fortunate hero in the sequel, because the central character is more experienced by that point. In *Jaws* (1975) the central character, Martin Brody, the new the chief of police of a small New England island town, loathes the ocean. By the end of that film, he has gone to sea and killed a massive man-eating shark. He still despises the ocean but has gained knowledge and experience. *Jaws 2* (1978) picks up four years later, and Brody is now a fortunate hero who must once again save the town from a giant shark.

Sometimes the second offering in a film series is a "distant sequel." In this case, the second story will take place many years after the first and the central character will mentor a new rising hero. For example, in *The Hustler* (1961) Paul Newman plays "Fast Eddie Felson" an up-and-coming pool player. 25 years later, Newman played Fast Eddie again in *The Color of Money* (1986), but this time he teaches a cocky but immensely talented protégé.

Sometimes a film will be an anthology of stories, such as *O. Henry's Full House* (1952), or *Creepshow* (1982). Even though these are single movies with multiple stories, they have a unifying device (frequently a host or narrator) to pull them together. Typically, the stories will at least have a common genre, if not a common theme.

O. Henry's Full House (1952)

There are many other ways of knitting multiple narratives together. A prequel, for example, is created subsequent to the original film, but has a narrative that takes place prior to the original film. *Butch Cassidy and the Sundance Kid* (1969) was made before *Butch and Sundance: The Early Day*s (1979). However, other examples, such as spin-offs, extended movie universes, franchises, reboots, revivals, remakes and even serials have plots that are typically independent of the original film.

Nearly every film plot will include some "plot devices." Plot devices are techniques (tricks of the trade) used to move the narrative forward. Some plot devices, such as the *deus ex machina*, are hallmarks of bad writing and make the audience feel cheated. Others can actually affirm the writer's duty to their audience.

Consider the paradigm of "Chekov's gun" which asserts that every element in a narrative must be necessary, and irrelevant elements should be removed. Offering advice to fellow authors, Anton Chekov said, if you hang a loaded rifle on a wall in the first act, in the second or third act it absolutely must go off or it shouldn't be there. On the other hand, sometimes a writer will offer up a "red herring" to achieve the opposite effect. The writer will purposely include extraneous things to surprise the audience.

In his book, *Ebert's Bigger Little Movie Glossary*, the great film critic Roger Ebert catalogs thousands of "movie clichés, stereotypes, obligatory scenes, hackneyed formulas, shopworn conventions, and outdated archetypes." It was compiled both as a challenge to spot recurring movie devices and as a way of examining how effective those devices are. A film narrative must be

31

extremely succinct, and production time and budget is very tight. The use of well-established conventions is almost obligatory. This does not necessarily make the plot weaker. In fact, plot devices are frequently used because they work.

For example, one of the most frequently used devices is the "MacGuffin." Popularized by director Alfred Hitchcock, a MacGuffin is a type of narrative device. Hitchcock described a MacGuffin in a lecture at Columbia University in 1939:

It might be a Scottish name, taken from a story about two men on a train. One man says, "What's that package up there in the baggage rack?" And the other answers, "Oh, that's a MacGuffin". The first one asks, "What's a MacGuffin?" "Well," the other man says, "it's an apparatus for trapping lions in the Scottish Highlands." The first man says, "But there are no lions in the Scottish Highlands," and the other one answers, "Well then, that's no MacGuffin!" So you see that a MacGuffin is actually nothing at all.

It frequently happens that the central character will be pursuing a thing of no consequence, a MacGuffin, which propels the narrative forward. The dramatic question will be about attaining an unimportant goal, and the central character will either fail in that quest or conclude that victory was unimportant. In the end, the MacGuffin will be largely forgotten, but something much more valuable will be attained. In *Rocky* (1976), Rocky Balboa is seeking the heavyweight boxing title. The title proves elusive in the end, but he wins the enduring love of his girlfriend, Adrian.

These are merely the basics of narrative, and accomplished writers and storytellers specialize in refining this model in unique and interesting ways. Some experts, such as Joseph Campbell, have exhaustively studied myths from many cultures, and have discovered commonalities not just in story arcs, but also in individual scenes. For example, the central character will frequently encounter a mentor character or will need to obtain some sort of amulet to complete his journey. In The Wizard of Oz (1939), Dorothy is required to get the witch's broom and bring it to the wizard. A deep understanding of the elements of myth can be a challenging but enormously useful skill for screenwriters.

Writers and other film artists may have varying interpretations of a narrative's structure, and it will fall to the director to align everyone involved behind a single vision. However, this task became routinized thanks to the efforts of Syd Field, a leading authority on screenwriting. Field's most significant contribution was the articulation of the "three-act structure."

In this paradigm, the first act roughly coincides with the first quarter of the film (30 minutes and 30 pages of a typical 120-page script). The first act usually includes everything from the point of attack through the hero's preparation for the journey. Most of the exposition will be out of the way, the inciting incident has occurred, and

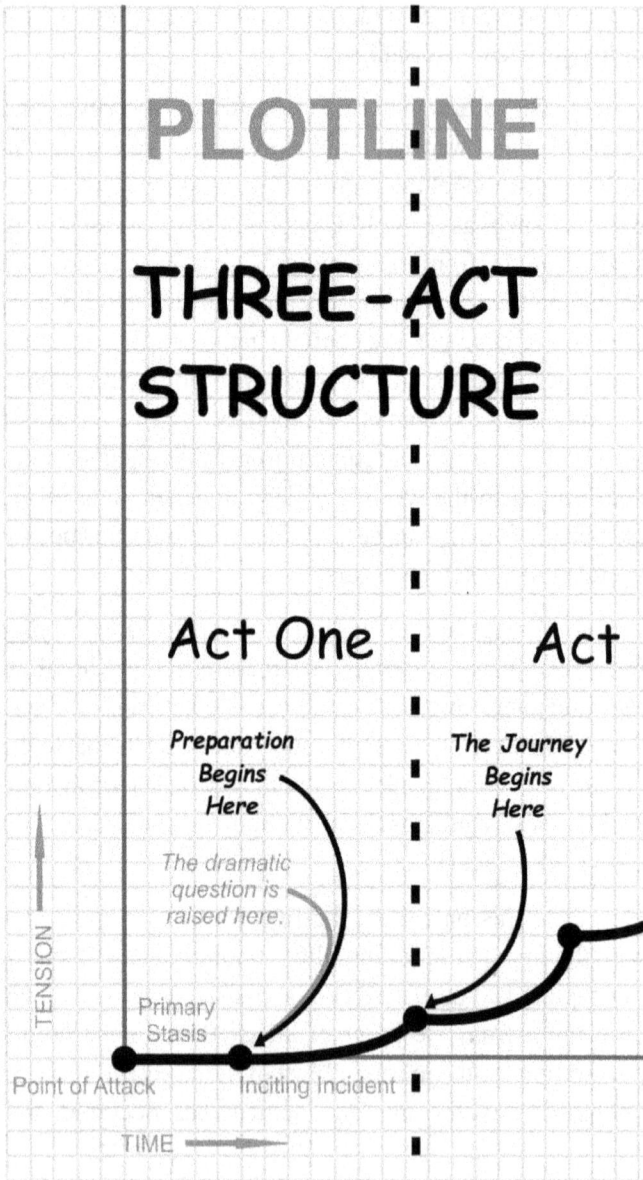

PLOTLINE

THREE-ACT STRUCTURE

Act One | Act

Preparation
Begins
Here

The Journey
Begins
Here

The dramatic
question is
raised here.

TENSION

Primary
Stasis

Point of Attack   Inciting Incident

TIME

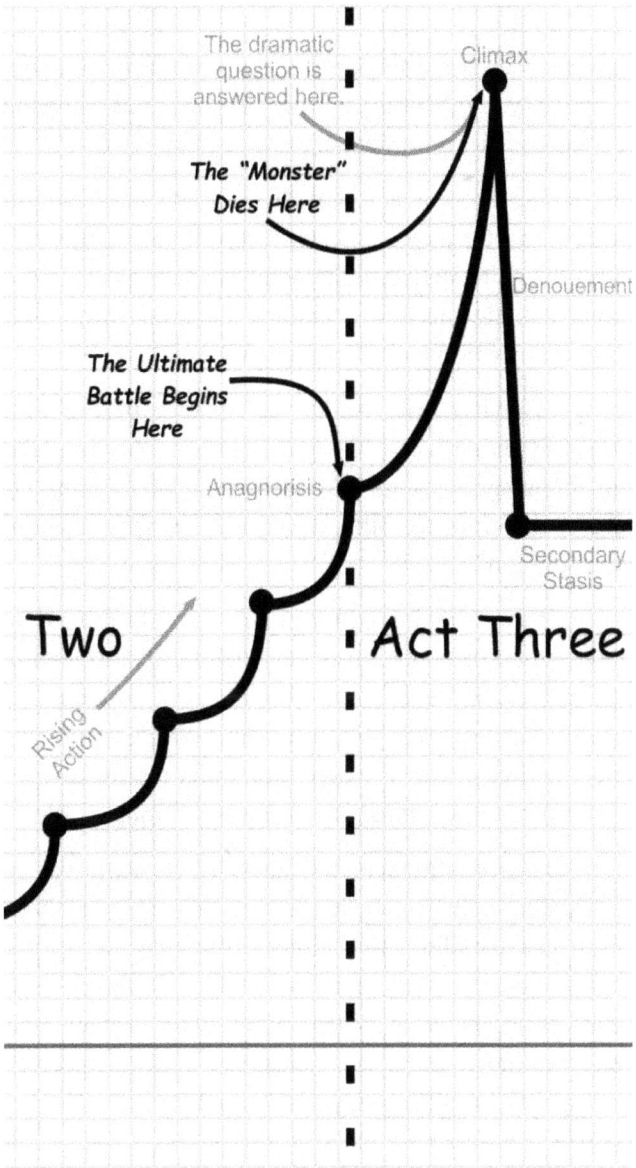

The dramatic question is answered here.

Climax

The "Monster" Dies Here

Denouement

The Ultimate Battle Begins Here

Anagnorisis

Secondary Stasis

Two

Act Three

Rising Action

there has been some sort of training and/or accumulation of necessary items for the journey. The act ends when the hero leaves his comfort zone.

The second act will be half of the film (60 minutes and 60 pages of a typical 120-page script). It covers the rising action to the point of anagnorisis. In the second act, the hero will endure numerous tests, and gather information and allies along the way.

The third act is the last quarter of the film (usually 30 minutes and 30 pages). This stretches from the point of anagnorisis to the final frame of the film. It includes the ultimate battle, the climax, the falling action and resolution.

Because major motion pictures are constructed by a large group of people, it is very helpful if everyone is cognizant of, and adheres to, this three-act structure. In fact, you can nearly set your watch by most contemporary major motion pictures; major plot shifts almost always happen at exactly 1/4 and 3/4 of the way through a film.

The construction and analysis of narratives is sport among some intellectuals, and their chimera is to find a new paradigm that either profoundly defies the rules or abides by them to perfection. Even the best narratives arguably leave room for improvement, and even the most contorted narratives find themselves drifting back to a classic mythical paradigm.

KEY POINTS:

- Aristotle was mistaken when he said that plot was the most important dramatic element.

- According to the paradigm of the *Rota Fortunae*, the fortunes of a central character will either rise, stay fortunate, fall, or remain unfortunate.

- The concept of the wheel of fortune originated in early agrarian societies when storytelling was a new idea.

- Those agrarian societies associated the four types of plot with the four seasons.

- While a central character may enjoy gains and endure setbacks within the narrative, it is the ultimate change in fortune that is significant.

- Narratives about unfortunate or rising heroes tend to be light-hearted, and narratives about fortunate or falling heroes tend to be more serious, **but** this is not always the case.

- A plotline is associated with a narrative, and not a story.

- A collection of plot points could be graphed, and a curve (or plot line) would connect those points.

- The X axis illustrates time, and the Y axis illustrates dramatic tension.
- The point of attack is at the origin.
- Primary stasis, or ordinary life, is where the plotline resides along the X axis.
- The inciting incident is on the Y axis but is some distance from the origin along the X axis.
- Critical exposition will happen during primary stasis.
- The inciting incident will set off a series of reactions that will raise the tension up the Y axis as time progresses across the X axis.
- The inciting incident will also give rise to a central question.
- The rising action will usually lead to a point of anagnorisis, a moment of profound discovery.
- Anagnorisis is a point of no return.
- Anagnorisis results in peripeteia, an abrupt turn of events, that sets the stage for the supreme ordeal.
- The climax is the point of maximum tension and where the central question is answered.
- When the monster is dead, the movie is over.
- Very little will happen after the climax and a secondary stasis will result.

- A *deus ex machina* is a character or object that comes out of nowhere to resolve the narrative.
- Occasionally a story will presage a sequel by introducing a new central question.
- A MacGuffin is a thing of no consequence, but the central character's pursuit of if it can nonetheless drive the narrative forward.
- There are many ways to analyze a plot, but Syd Field's three-act structure has become standard in filmmaking.
- Plots can be manipulated in unlimited ways but will invariably adhere to basic narrative principles.

CHAPTER THREE
DIALOGUE

Film is a visual medium, and filmmakers concur that showing is better than telling. This can be misconstrued however. While it's certainly better to see action played out than to be told about it, it doesn't mean that dialogue should be dispensed with, or that it necessarily weakens a film. If that were the case, silent movies would still be popular. In fact, in the 1920's some producers regarded sound film as an unnecessary fad, but obviously audiences felt differently. Of course, dialogue is best when it is accompanied with fitting visuals. As with all the dramatic elements, the use of dialogue isn't a question of right or wrong, but rather a question of appropriateness and balance.

For example, in *Casablanca* (1942), the central character, Rick Blaine, gets sentimental about a romance he had some years previous in Paris. Rather than describe the affair, he gets drunk, and his memories play out in a lengthy flashback. On the other hand, in *Mr. Smith Goes to Washington* (1939), Mr. Smith gives a long, impassioned speech about corruption as he filibusters in the U.S. Senate. During the scene, the packed senate chamber is absolutely motionless as he assiduously pleads his case until he collapses on the floor from exhaustion. The visuals work well in Casablanca because it's a more satisfying and detailed way of filling in exposition, but the speech in *Mr. Smith Goes to Washington* works equally well because it's suited to the action of the scene. The audience is gripped by Mr. Smith's quixotic attempt to persuade the senators.

Mr. Smith Goes to Washington (1939)

The choice of showing or telling in a film is not binary; it lies on a spectrum. The fact that film is more visual than literature, music, or radio doesn't mean that dialogue isn't a great way to enhance the narrative of a film. Like cooking, the art of filmmaking is about finding the perfect blend of ingredients to achieve the desired outcome.

Dialogue fulfills many functions in a film. Not only can it reveal exposition and express the theme, but it can also further the plot, establish the tone, entertain with humor, and inform with facts. Perhaps most importantly, dialogue can create conflict, and conflict propels a narrative forward. Of course, all those things could be done without dialogue, but dialogue is frequently the most elegant solution.

It's often said that good dialogue needs to be "realistic," but that's a very slippery term when it comes to any artistic endeavor. In the "real world" people are painfully inarticulate. It would be more accurate to say that dialogue needs to be honest and appropriate. For example, dialogue written for a child may use limited vocabulary and shorter sentences. The language of a coal miner would likely be coarser than the language of an elementary school teacher. However, there may be times when uncharacteristic dialogue could be used for effect. For example, in *Airplane!* (1980), an elegant suburban housewife (played by the quintessential "TV mom," Barbara Billingsley) translates the "jive talk" of two other airplane passengers for comic effect.

Attndnt

Can I get you something?

Jivemn2

S'mo fo butter layin' to the bone.
Jackin' me up. Tightly.

Attndnt

I'm sorry I don't understand.

Jivemn1

Cutty say he cant hang.

Woman4

Oh stewardess, I speak jive.

Attndnt

Ohhhh, good.

Woman4

He said that he's in great pain and he
wants to know if you can help him.

Attndnt

Would you tell him to just relax and
I'll be back as soon as I can with
some medicine.

Woman4

Jus' hang loose blooood. She goonna
catch up on the`rebound a de medcide.

Jivemn2

What it is big mamma, my mamma didn't
raise no dummy, I dug her rap.

```
Woman4

Cut me som' slac' jak! Chump don wan
no help, chump don git no help. Jive
ass dude don got no brains anyhow.
```

Airplane! (1980)

In some ways, dialogue is not realistic at all. While we accept many conventions in film as realistic, nearly everything about it is pretense, and dialogue is no exception. Characters are far wittier and succinct on screen than people are in real life. Characters rarely say completely irrelevant things; they usually say exactly what is necessary to move the narrative forward.

Great movie quotes are especially succinct, and well-timed. They're profound within the context of the narrative. For example, in the film *The Wizard of Oz* (1939), the central character, Dorothy, and her dog Toto,

The Wizard of Oz (1939)

are swept up by a tornado from their dull black-and-white Kansas farm, and are transported to a beautiful Technicolor Munchkinland. Bewildered, Dorothy utters the iconic line, "Toto, I've a feeling we're not in Kansas anymore." Upon greater scrutiny, it's not very profound in terms of its explicit meaning, but its implicit meaning is significant. Most people are literally "not in Kansas," and the importance of that is quite inconsequential. On the other hand, the understatement of Dorothy's subtext is huge. The point isn't that Toto and Dorothy have been transported from their dull Kansas home, but that they have landed in a wondrous yet disconcerting place. The alarming thing is where they are, not where they aren't.

That line (and the perfect delivery by Judy Garland) resonates in the hearts of every viewer, most of whom have never been to Kansas or Munchkinland, but have found themselves unnervingly out of their comfort zone. It immediately evokes a feeling of sympathetic recognition. In fact, the line has found its way into cultural literacy and common parlance and is frequently quoted when one lands in an uncomfortable situation.

The power of great dialogue is not in exotic word choice, but rather the specificity, conciseness, context, and appropriateness of the words. Great script writers labor over every syllable. However, while scripts for stage plays are treated with reverence, and dialogue is never changed without the permission of the playwright, this is not the case for screen plays. For example, in *Star Wars: Episode V - The Empire Strikes Back* (1980), Princess

Leia confesses her love to Han Solo, who is facing execution and the script reads like this:

> (He takes her in his arms and
> she gives him a passionate
> kiss.)
>
> ### LEIA
>
> ... I love you. I couldn't tell
> you before, but it's true.
>
> ### HAN
>
> ... just remember that, 'cause
> I'll be back...
>
> (He sheds his cocky smile and
> gives her a soft kiss on the
> forehead. Tears roll down Leia's
> face as she watches the dashing
> pirate walk to the hydraulic
> platform.)

However, when the cast and crew went to shoot the scene, they knew it was awkward. So the director, producer, and actors, began to rewrite it – without consulting the screenwriters. The final scene goes like this:

(He leans in for a passionate
kiss before being dragged away
to the hydraulic platform.)

LEIA

... I love you.

HAN

I know.

(He is slowly lowered into the
carbonite pit.)

The words couldn't be simpler. "I love you" has been said countless times through the millennia, but the simple response within the context of the situation is striking. Why doesn't he respond with "I love you too?" Does he love her? Does he think it will spare her feelings if she thinks he doesn't love her? Is he really so egotistical that he assumes everyone loves him? In any case, the ambiguity of the response is eloquently captivating.

Star Wars: Episode V - The Empire Strikes Back (1980)

49

Some directors will encourage actors to improvise their dialogue. Rather than adhering to a script with carefully chosen words, it's reasonable to conclude that it would be more "realistic" to have actors speak naturally. While some directors, such as Woody Allen, have had success with this, it's not always efficacious. It can muddle the narrative by filling the dialogue with extraneous words and often causes actors to interrupt and talk over each other. While improvisation does have a natural feel, it works against the idea of film as a visual medium. It tends to make films more labored and talky.

The extreme example of improvised dialogue can be found in "mumblecore" films such as *Funny Ha Ha* (2002). Mumblecore is a twenty-first century style of filmmaking that has its roots in the twentieth century cinéma vérité and method acting. It emphasizes "honesty" over narrative. Mumblecore films are created on an extremely low budget, often using amateur artists and equipment as well as improvised dialogue. This becomes a technical nightmare for sound and editing, giving mumblecore it's moniker. The dialogue is extremely prosaic and moves the narrative at a snail's pace, but it's earnest and it authentically reflects the experience of the millennial generation.

On the other hand, when filmmakers give up all pretense of pretense, it too can be construed as honest. When a film is self-aware and acknowledges its own artifice, it's ironically truthful.

Funny Ha Ha (2002)

There is a conceptual "fourth wall" between the audience and the world of the film that keeps the audience at a metaphorical safe distance. The term "fourth wall" comes from live theater where "realistic" stories often take place in a single room. The stage set has only three walls, and there is an implied fourth wall between the audience and the stage. Should an actor come downstage and directly address the audience, it would be as if he were talking right through the fourth wall.

The use of a narrator in film breaks that fourth wall concept and dispels the illusion of a discreet universe. A narrator (or even title cards in a silent film) simultaneously pulls an audience into the story and reminds them that it's all make-believe. However, the use of narration and title cards have become such a common convention in film that they rarely disrupt the suspension of disbelief. Only when an on-screen character speaks directly to the audience is the effect disquieting. For example, in *Ferris Bueller's Day Off* (1986) the central character speaks directly to the cinema audience throughout the film. In fact, after the ending credits, he looks straight into the camera and addresses the movie audience one last time. "You're still here?" he asks. "It's over. Go home. Go."

Dialogue fails most often when a character says something without being honestly motivated to say it. This happens frequently when a screenwriter inartfully attempts to deliver exposition to the audience. Infamously in the film, *Big Hero Six* (2014), Tadashi plaintively asks

Ferris Bueller's Day Off (1986)

his brother, "What would Mom and Dad say?" and his brother, Hiro, replies "I don't know. They're gone. They died when I was three, remember?" Yes, it's likely that his brother remembers that their parents are dead, but now, thanks to painfully awkward dialogue, the audience is aware of it too. This is referred to as "as you know" dialogue. Other variants of "as you know" dialogue include "tell me about it professor" dialogue, "maid and butler" dialogue, "new guy" dialogue, "pour your guts out to the bartender (or psychiatrist)" dialogue, "read the letter out loud" dialogue, and "explain it to the sidekick" dialogue. While audiences will usually accept these conventions, it detracts from the believability of a film.

A similar thing frequently happens at the end of a film when either the antagonist or the protagonist explains at length what really happened in the film. The verbose antagonist, often holding the hero at gunpoint, will delight in discussing the events of the narrative rather than dispatching with the hero, who now has time to work a way out of his predicament. In a similar fashion, it has become almost customary for a detective in a "who-done-it" to gather all the suspects together at the end of the story and explain at length how it all really happened.

It's hardly a spoiler to learn that the central character in *Psycho* (1960) is a psychopath. Nonetheless, after the climax of the film, with the central character already confined to a mental hospital, the audience is infamously given a nearly five-minute long explanation of what happened by a new character, a psychiatrist.

Listed in the credits as Dr. Fred Richman, the psychiatrist was played by Simon Oakland and was referred to as "Simon" in the script. This is a clear indication that this new character had no backstory. He was just a sort of deus ex machina brought in to explain away some plot holes as the rest of the characters look on.

```
               SIMON

          (interrupting)

    As I said, the mother...

          (Pauses, goes on afresh)

    To understand it, as I
    understood it hearing it from
    the mother...That is, from the
    mother-half of Norman's mind,
    you have to go back ten years...
    to the time when Norman murdered
    his mother and her lover.
```

(A pause, then as no one
interrupts)

He was already dangerously
disturbed, had been ever since
his father died. His mother was
a clinging, demanding woman...
and for years the two of them
lived as if there was no one
else in the world. Then she met
a man and it seemed to Norman
she "threw him over" for this
man. That pushed him over the
thin line... and he killed them
both. Matricide is probably the
most unbearable crime of all...
and most unbearable to the son
who commits it. So he had to
erase the crime, at least in his
own mind.

(A pause)

He stole her corpse... and a
weighted coffin was buried. He
hid the body in the fruit
cellar, even "treated" it to
keep it as well as it would
keep. And that still wasn't
enough. She was there, but she
was a corpse. So he began to
think and speak for her, gave
her half his life, so to speak.
At times he could be both
personalities, carry on
conversations... at other times,
the mother-half took over

completely. He was never all Norman, but he was often only mother. And because he was so pathologically jealous of her, he assumed she was as jealous of him. Therefore, if he felt a strong attraction to any other woman, the mother side of him would go wild.

           (To Lila)

When Norman met your sister, he was touched by her... and aroused by her. He wanted her. And this set off his "jealous mother" and... "mother killed the girl." After the murder, Norman returned as if from a deep sleep... and like a dutiful son, covered up all traces of the crime he was convinced his mother had committed.

             SAM

Why was he... dressed like that?

        DISTRICT ATTORNEY

He's a transvestite!

           SIMON

Not exactly. A man who dresses in woman's clothing in order to achieve a sexual change... or satisfaction... is a transvestite. But in Norman's case, he was simply doing everything possible to keep alive the illusion of his mother being alive. And whenever reality came too close, when danger or desire threatened that illusion, he'd dress up, even to a cheap wig he brought, and he'd walk about the house, sit in her chair, speak in her voice... He tried to be his mother.

(A sad smile)

And now he is.

(A pause)

That's what I meant when I said I got the story from the mother. She thinks Norman has been taken away... because of his crimes. She insists she did nothing, that Norman committed all the murders just to keep her from being discovered. She even smiled a bit coquettishly as she said that. Of course, she feels badly about it... but also somewhat relieved to be, as she put it, free of Norman, at last.

(A pause)

> When the mind houses two
> personalities, there is always a
> battle. In Norman's case, the
> battle is over... and the
> dominant personality has won.

Dialogue is neither a good nor a bad thing, but merely one element of film. The absence of dialogue is also very important; often, less is more. Great word choice and subtext can also be a potent way to drive the narrative. Ultimately, dialogue must blend with the other elements to form the perfect narrative mix.

KEY POINTS:

- The amount of dialogue in a film is less significant than the quality and appropriateness of the dialogue.
- Dialogue should supplement but not replace the visual elements.
- Dialogue is often the easiest way to create conflict and propel a narrative forward.
- It is a convention that film dialogue is more clever, succinct and relevant than naturalistic dialogue.
- Great movie quotes are especially succinct, well-timed, and packed with subtext.

- While lengthy speeches can be effective, because of the time constraints of film, short, pithy dialogue is usually more powerful.
- Subtext can be as evocative as the text.
- Improvised or naturalistic dialogue may seem more honest, but it can slow the pace of a film and be difficult to edit.
- Narration is an efficient way to reveal a character's thoughts and pull an audience into the world of the film.
- Narration can also be alienating because it reminds an audience they are watching a film.
- Characters, such as "the new guy" are often introduced to motivate expository dialogue.
- The denouement of a film can be burdened by excessive dialogue necessary to explain what the film failed to illustrate.
- The absence of dialogue can be as powerful as the dialogue itself.

CHAPTER FOUR

THEME

Standard advice for screen writers has always been that "If you want to send a message, call Western Union." It's unclear who first made that observation, but surely it was a producer who regarded the element of theme as frivolous. On the other hand, others would argue that theme is the most important element because it's the reason for making and watching a film. Theme is all about the message.

Aristotle believed that all dramas should have a unity of time, place, and action. He suggested that for a drama to be believable, the narrative must not only occur within a single place and in real time, but it must also be about a single idea. Since Aristotle's day, audiences have accepted the convention of moving through space and time in a narrative, but only to a limited extent. The general concept of Aristotle's unities persists. One would not expect to see a contemporary romantic comedy, suddenly shift into a futuristic sci-fi thriller, and then turn into a Civil War epic. Generally speaking, well-made films will occur in a single time and place. They will also generally be centered on a single major theme. There may be secondary themes associated with subplots, but a film focused on a jumble of themes will seem random and unsatisfying. Bringing focus to a narrative – giving it a single objective – may be the most important attribute of a strong theme.

Themes can range from something very basic, such as "crime doesn't pay" or "love conquers all," to something more complex such as "desire leads to despair." Themes are never simply a topic such as "family," "home," or "money." Because themes send a message, they must take a position on those topics. "Families are toxic." "Returning home is inevitable." "Money will corrupt the purest of heart."

Theme is frequently confused with other concepts. A narrative theme is not like a party theme. A toga party will have people dressed as bacchanals, a masquerade will have everyone wearing masks, and a baby shower might have yellow duckies galore, but that's more about style (see the chapter on tone) than about a message.

Sometimes theme is confused with conflict. Concepts such as "man vs. nature," "good vs. evil," or "power vs. humility" reference the plot, and are not themes. Obviously, the plot and the theme will be necessarily related. For example, the theme of a "man vs. nature" film might be "man is powerless before nature," but it could just as easily be something like "nature must yield to the ingenuity of man." Simply identifying the conflict in the story isn't as useful as identifying the message of the story. Themes must take a position on a subject.

Theme shouldn't be confused with genre either. Genre is a way of classifying films. Labels such as "horror," "western," or "sci-fi" are useful for researching or marketing films, but they aren't themes.

Themes are unifying devices, but not all unifying devices are themes. While the theme is most apparent at the climax of a film, when the central character (and by extension the audience) has learned a lesson, in more complex narratives the theme will be evident throughout the plot and subplots, and will take the form of a motif. Given that narratives are focused on a single message, it isn't surprising that unity is created when the message is grappled with repeatedly over the course of a film. For example, in *The Lord of the Rings* trilogy (2001, 2002, 2003) the corrupting effects of power are played out repeatedly by various characters until it becomes a unifying device throughout the films.

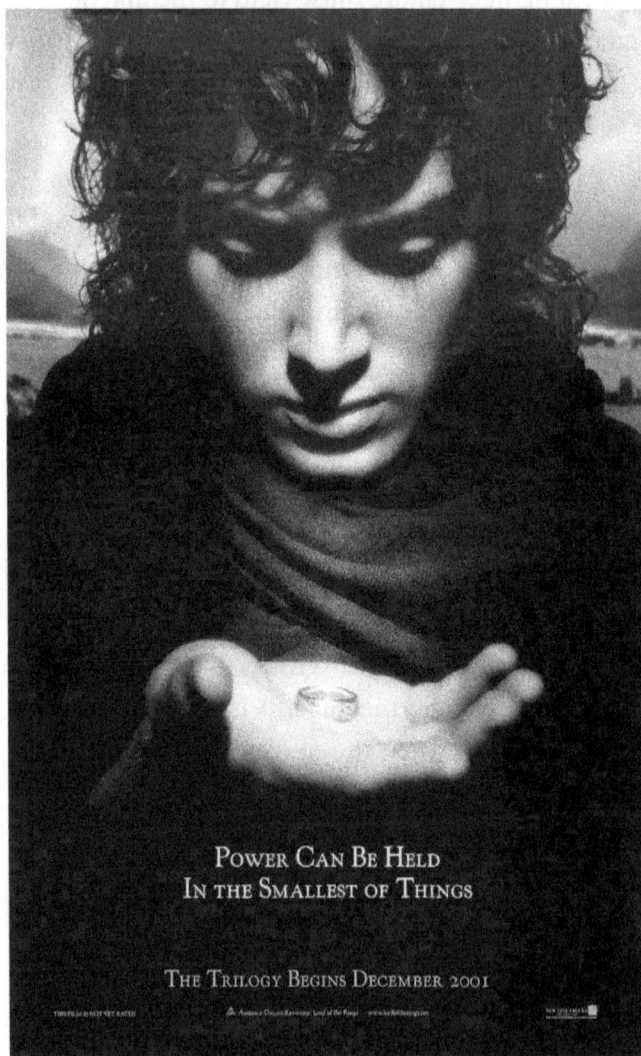

POWER CAN BE HELD
IN THE SMALLEST OF THINGS

THE TRILOGY BEGINS DECEMBER 2001

The Lord of the Rings: The Fellowship of the Ring (2001)

However, not every unifying device is related to theme. For example, clocks are a prominent motif in *High Noon* (1952). They add suspense about the impending midday gunfight, but the theme of the film has nothing to do with clocks or time. In *Close Encounters of the Third Kind* (1977) a string of five musical notes pervades the film and give it unity, but the film isn't about music. Motifs create unity and mood, but they aren't themes.

High Noon (1952)

Themes are often straightforward and expected. In most westerns or crime dramas "the good guys win," and most romantic comedies will see "love conquer all." These are simplistic themes and an audience will accept them without much thought. Theme is not a dominant element in those sorts of narratives. Other films (particularly documentaries) will be more thought provoking. They seek to enlighten their audiences, and theme will be a significant element in the narrative. The film *1984* (1956), for example, explores how "rebellion naturally devolves into totalitarianism." When a filmmaker really does want to send a message, theme will be the most important element.

Other times filmmakers eschew messages. Action films are more about spectacle than theme, and their producers don't expect that audiences will leave the theater more enlightened than when they came in.

On the other hand, filmmakers sometimes embrace controversial themes as a way of targeting an audience. The Oscar-winning *Cider House Rules* (1999) for example, makes a clear argument in favor of abortion. While the film is hailed by some, it is decried by others. Usually producers will avoid controversy for fear of alienating half of their potential audience. For them, Western Union remains a better way to send a message.

Some postmodern filmmakers will go out of their way to avoid anything that could be construed as a message at all in an apparent protest of the concept of aesthetics. They prefer serendipity and randomness over making a statement. Nonetheless, avoiding theme entirely is impossible, and in the end, these films make a statement about randomness and a disdain for the rules of aesthetics anyway.

Theoretically a film could be made in such a random fashion that it would have no theme at all, but a film with no purpose is also bereft of communication because it has nothing to communicate. Many films fail because they have nothing to say, and in the end, the audience is uncertain why they bothered to watch the film. Style, genre, conflict, or motifs are no substitute for taking a position on a subject.

KEY POINTS:

- The message that's being sent by a narrative is the theme.
- Aristotle believed that if a narrative is to be believable, it should occur in real time, in a single place, and deliver a single message.

- It remains true that while a narrative might include a number of smaller themes, a good narrative will center on a single main theme.

- Because themes need to send a message, they must be more than a simple topic; they must take a position on a topic.

- Themes should not be confused with genre, conflict, style, or tone.

- Themes form a motif when they are reinforced in multiple ways within a narrative. However, not all motifs are themes.

- Themes can be straightforward or thought-provoking and complex. They can be controversial or universal. They can even be muddled to the point of confusion, but narratives always make some sort of statement.

CHAPTER FIVE

CHARACTER

A narrative would never progress without the actions of characters. If a plot is a series of reactions to actions, then someone or something must be doing all of that reacting. For that reason, plot is never more important than the characters that drive it.

Narratives will always focus on the experience of a central character, and the audience, having empathy for that character, will experience the narrative with them. Theoretically, the best possible narrative will evoke the greatest amount of empathy for its central character. This is why we jump when the central character is startled by a monster, or cheer when he scores the winning point, or cry when he succumbs to an incurable disease. We go on a journey with the central character and maybe even psychologically become the central character.

On the other hand, the audience's experience isn't genuine. No one in the audience is actually threatened by a monster, scoring the winning point, or contracting an incurable disease. The audience learns vicariously what it might be like if those things were to happen, which is both easier and safer than actually going through the experience. Suppose, for example, you wanted to know if it's a good idea to alleviate your boredom and lack of money by involving your girlfriend and family members in a series of high-stakes bank heists. You could literally talk your family into robbing some banks, or you might simply watch the film *Bonnie and Clyde* (1967). Certainly, watching a movie is a meager analogue of going on an actual crime spree, but it's a lot more rational. Unlike the central characters in the film, the audience has an ersatz experience, but done well, it's nonetheless involving, emotional, and instructive.

Bonnie and Clyde (1967)

The central character is also known as the "protagonist," a term that comes from the ancient Greek theatre, and literally means "first contender (or combatant)." Greek theatre began as a religious ceremony, where a chorus would lecture an audience by singing or chanting to them. Legend has it that at some point a performer (supposedly named Thespis) stepped out front and began a dialogue with the chorus. This is why actors are sometimes referred to as "thespians." Thespis became the first protagonist, and was soon followed by two other performers, the deuteragonist and the tritagonist. It was the job of the protagonist to give voice to the audience, question the chorus, and react to the deuteragonist and the tritagonist. It would be more than 2,500 years before the protagonist found his way to film, but he still represents the audience.

There are four types of protagonists (central characters or heroes). Each is associated with one of the four basic plots. The comic, or rising, hero encourages us to fight a worthy fight and convinces us that we can one day attain our greatest desire. The romantic, or fortunate, hero deepens our belief in great virtues such as truth, justice, charity, and patience. The tragic, or falling, hero's story is a cautionary tale. He warns us about the danger of arrogance and teaches us humility. Finally, the ironic, or unfortunate, hero teaches us that anything that can go wrong will go wrong, and we must endure life with a sense of humor.

Comic and romantic heroes are often reluctant heroes. While tragic and ironic heroes will foolishly take on a challenge unprepared for the consequences, comic and romantic heroes will often resist taking up a challenge for as long as possible. Hubris frequently defeats the tragic and ironic heroes, while humility is the saving grace of the comic and romantic heroes.

Sometimes a protagonist is an antihero, a character that does the right thing for the wrong reasons. The term "anti-hero" can be a little confusing. This is not the antagonist. An anti-hero is a central character, aligned with the "unfortunate hero" on the Rota Fortunae. Instead of being a powerful fortunate hero who saves the day time after time – like Superman, he is unfortunate. Even though he may be skilled, he is often depressed and the struggles with the challenges of everyday life. Unlike his comedic unfortunate counterpart (for example, Charlie Chaplin's "Little Tramp") who shrugs off setbacks and tries again, the anti-hero becomes more and more cynical over time. He is a terribly flawed but somehow sympathetic character. In the end, the anti-hero will resolve the dramatic question, but will remain dissatisfied on a deeper level. For example, in *Dirty Harry* (1971), Harry Callahan is a disgruntled police inspector who lives in an imperfect world and feels justified in breaking the rules to suit his own moral code. Though his actions border on reprehensible at times, he remains sympathetic because the audience acknowledges that he is doing a thankless job.

It's also worth noting that the central character could be more than one person. Buddy pictures and romantic comedies often have more than one central character. However, the fates of these characters are inextricably tied and the trajectory of their combined fates (rising, falling, or staying the same) will be identical. For example, in *Thelma and Louise* (1991), two desperate women from Arkansas go on the run together from the

Detective Harry Callahan.

You don't
assign
him to
murder
cases.

You just
turn him loose.

Clint Eastwood
Dirty Harry

Dirty Harry (1971)

police, and ultimately endure the same fate. If the fate of two characters runs in opposition to each other, one is likely the protagonist (central character) and the other is an antagonist.

When animals, places, or inanimate objects are the focus of a story, they are more likely to be MacGuffins than actual central characters. In *Seabiscut* (2003), the titular racehorse wins the day, but the audience identifies with his jockey, and in *The Maltese Falcon* (1941), everyone is after the jewel-encrusted falcon statuette, but detective Sam Spade is clearly the central character and not the falcon.

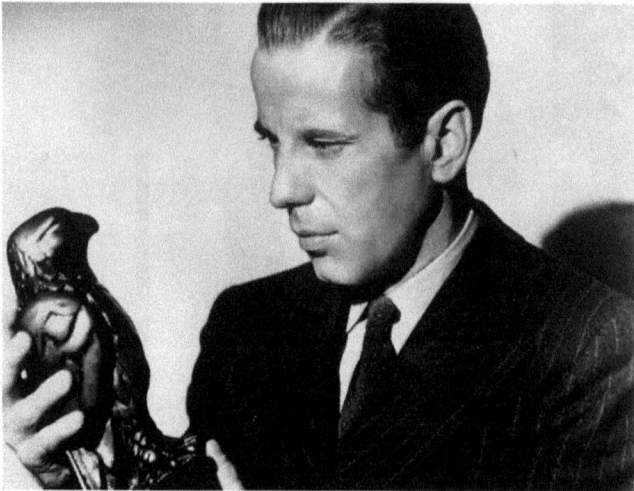

The Maltese Falcon (1941)

Even in a true "ensemble" film, one character will stand out as a protagonist. This is often in seen in disaster films or heist films. For example, in *Sneakers* (1992),

Martin Bishop (played by Robert Redford) distinguishes himself as the leader of a group of 6 experts who specialize in testing security systems. While the whole group has a common goal and their trajectory is the same, in the end, Redford's character has a unique fate. Another example is *Earthquake* (1974). There are more than 40 actors with speaking roles in the film, but Charlton Heston, playing construction engineer Stuart Graff, establishes himself as the central character, even with relatively little screen time, because at some point, his character interacts with each of the other characters.

Sometimes (particularly in documentaries) the theme can be the central character. For example, in the documentary *Bully* (2001), the concept of bullying in schools is the central character. While there were more than 30 people (kids and adults) featured in the film, they served to represent different facets of the theme. In allegorical films, the characters may directly portray concepts. For example, in Ingmar Bergman's *The Seventh Seal* (1957) a knight, representing "life", and the grim reaper, representing death, play a game of chess.

Nearly all the characters in a fictional narrative will line up on one of two sides. They will either help the protagonist in his quest to resolve the dramatic question, or they will stand in the protagonist's way. However, in some movies like, *Stalag 17* (1953) or *Force 10 from Navarone* (1978), or *The League of Extraordinary Gentlemen* (2003), characters will switch sides or be double agents.

Typically, a protagonist will have a well-defined antagonist (a Greek word meaning competitor or opponent) of equivalent or superior ability. Antagonists can be a group of people, animals, institutions, objects, or even the protagonist himself. When the protagonist and antagonist are the same character they often have a mental health problem and are battling inner demons. For example, in *A Beautiful Mind* (2001), mathematician John Nash (played by Russel Crowe), must fight to keep a grip on reality as he suffers the destructive nature of schizophrenia.

The Little Mermaid (1989)

Beyond the protagonist and antagonist, a narrative will have a cast of allies and enemies. The protagonist usually relies on supporting characters to help him find his way, and the antagonist will have his henchman too. However, the allies and enemies have limited abilities and will sometimes even be counterproductive. In fact, a well-meaning ally might tempt the protagonist to cheat, take shortcuts, or give up on the quest altogether. Likewise, an inept henchman might snarl the plans of the antagonist. These characters are sometimes referred to as "contagonists." For example, in *The Little Mermaid* (1989) Ariel, the little mermaid, dreams of visiting the world above the water, but her friend Sebastian, a crab, tries with a song to persuade her that things are better "Under the Sea."

Characters are defined by their actions. We know who they are by what they do. When we say an actor is playing a role, it refers not only to the name of the character, but the function of that character in the narrative. It is also why characters should be construed as archetypes, and not stereotypes. There are endless character archetypes in narratives, such as the mentor, the trickster, or the guardian character, but they are always described by their function. On the other hand, a stereotype (a word that originally meant a printed copy of something) relies on surface-level descriptions that are frequently derogatory. Archetypes focus on verbs (a character's behavior), which is what drives a good narrative. Stereotypes focus on adjectives (what characters appear to be). If a storyteller emphasizes stereotypes over archetypes, the narrative will fall flat because it isn't propelled forward via action. For example, in *Breakfast at Tiffany's* (1961), Mr. Yunioshi, the central character's Japanese neighbor, is undeniably played in such a stereotypical fashion that it unnecessarily ruins an otherwise excellent film.

There have been many systems of character paradigms through the centuries. For example, the ancients had their classical myths, and religions have their parables. Think of Achilles or Gilgamesh. Fables and fairy tales have early roots as well. Consider Chicken Little or Red Riding Hood. The theatre is another repository of archetypal figures. Look at Oedipus or King Lear. Further, the adoption of the printing press brought us a long line of literary archetypes. (Think of everyone from Robinson Crusoe to Superman.) In more recent years, psychologists, sociologists, gaming, television, and film have all employed systems of archetypes.

Many have tried to codify these systems. Early on, Saint John the Ascetic described archetypes related to the seven deadly sins and seven heavenly virtues in his book *De Institutis Coenobiorum* ("Institutes"). During the Italian Renaissance, Flaminio Scala recorded the improvised narratives and stock characters of the *Commedia dell' Arte* in his book, *Il Teatro delle Favole Rappresentative*. Carl Jung took a psychoanalytical approach to the subject in his collected essays, *The Archetypes and The Collective Unconscious*. Mythologist, Joseph Campbell, discussed the topic in detail in his many books including, *The Hero with a Thousand Faces*. More recently the internet has been used as an aggregator of character archetypes. For example, the TV Tropes website (http://tvtropes.org/), a pop culture wiki, lists more than 100 archetypes. It is likely that there are an infinite number of archetypes imaginable, though frequently the most effective are the classical archetypes that have been seen again and again in the various systems.

Consider the "mentor" character for example. The function of the mentor (recall that archetypes are defined by what they do) is to train the hero. There have been many mentor characters throughout history (Athena, Merlin, Sir John Falstaff, Gandalf, Yoda, Mr. Miyagi, Dumbledore, etc.), and it is precisely because the mentor archetype is so familiar that it quickly resonates with the audience with very little explanation.

Daniel and Mr. Miyagi in *The Karate Kid* (1984)

On the other hand, each mentor character will be distinct because each has a different look, personality, or method of mentoring. In fact, the more extraordinary the character traits are, the more endearing, and believable, the characters are. Athena, Falstaff, and Yoda may serve the same narrative function, but their look, their speech, their backstory, their intellect, their abilities, their morals, their ethics, and everything else about them is distinct and memorable.

Some novice writers try to avoid the use of archetypes for fear that their characters will be predictable or flat, but avoiding the use of archetypes is pretty much impossible because archetypes are defined not by their stereotypical outward appearance but by their actions. For example, suppose a writer wants to include a "threshold guardian" archetype in their story. This is a character that must be appeased or dealt with in some fashion before the protagonist can proceed. Let us also suppose that the setting for this story is backwoods Mississippi. It would be stereotypical to include a fat middle-age police sheriff that menaces from behind mirrored sunglasses. However, suppose the sheriff were instead a small redheaded woman toting a long sword, the complete works of Henry Wadsworth Longfellow, and a peppermint mocha? She would be far more interesting than the stereotypical sheriff character, but she could still fill the archetypal role of the threshold guardian.

One of the worst mistakes a novice writer can make is to employ an "everyman" character. The idea of the everyman is that he's so generic that every audience member, regardless of their background, will be able to identify with the character. This always ends with a flat, uninteresting character with whom no one can identify. Ironically, it is the specificity of a character that creates universal appeal.

Other classic archetypes include the barefoot sage, pirate, blind seer, champion, miser, whore-with-a-heart-of-gold, cynic, dragon-slayer, drunk, muscle, braggart soldier, chosen one, madam, ferryman, jester, gentle giant, benevolent king, trickster, granny, herald, ambitious queen, grotesque, hunter, scout, loner, klutz, rogue, Mary Sue, bureaucrat, born loser, knight in shining armor, girl next door, inept doctor, patriarch, rebel, bloviating academic, Pollyanna, shadow, Prince Charming, shapeshifter, threshold guardian, star-crossed lover, foreigner, novice, wicked stepmother, artist, enabler, feminist, innocent, boss, femme fatale, imposter, reprobate, shaman, intellect, righteous reformer, narcissist, raisonneur, zombie, pessimist, and infinitely more.

Characters generally remain true to their type. For example, a benevolent king will not suddenly turn evil, and a loner won't suddenly be gregarious. Even when the change is motivated by a plot point, audiences will be distrustful of a character who suddenly changes type. This is frequently seen in films such as *Primal Fear* (1996) where a character has a dissociative identity (multiple personality) disorder, or when some sort of magic spell or potion changes a character's personality as in *The Mask* (1994). A "changeling" archetype will be mercurial, but that's in their archetypal nature. Protagonists will change substantially over the course of a film, but this will happen slowly, and must be motivated by the action of the film.

KEY POINTS:

- Characters drive the action of a narrative.
- Narratives focus on the journey of the central character.
- The audience vicariously experiences the narrative with the central character.
- "Protagonist" is a Greek term meaning "first contender."
- The "deuteragonist" and the "tritagonist" are the second and third contenders.
- There are four types of heroes: rising (comic), fortunate (romantic), falling (tragic), and unfortunate (ironic).
- Rising and fortunate heroes are often reluctant, but falling and unfortunate heroes are often foolhardy.
- An antihero is a terribly flawed but somehow sympathetic character who becomes more cynical over time as the narrative progresses.
- If there is more than one central character (such as in a buddy picture) the trajectory of their fate will be the same – rising, fortunate, falling, or unfortunate.
- If the fates of two characters run in opposition to each other, one is likely a protagonist and the other is an antagonist.
- Animals, places, or inanimate objects are more likely MacGuffins than central characters.
- Sometimes (particularly in documentaries) concepts can be the central character.

- In allegories, the central characters will represent concepts.
- Nearly all characters will be either aiding the protagonist or thwarting him.
- A character may switch sides or be a double agent.
- The antagonist will have equivalent or superior ability compared to the protagonist.
- Antagonists can be a group of people, animals, institutions, objects, or even the protagonist himself.
- The protagonist and antagonist usually have allies and henchmen respectively, but those characters will have limited abilities.
- An ally or henchman who is counterproductive is called a contagonist.
- Characters are defined by their actions.
- Characters should be construed as archetypes – distinguished by their role in the narrative.
- Characters should not be construed as stereotypes - defined by their appearance.
- There have been many systems of character paradigms through the centuries.
- Archetypes resonate with an audience with very little need for explanation.
- Specificity will make functionally similar archetypes distinct.
- "Everyman" characters are flat and uninteresting.

- Archetypal characters will remain constant to their type, unless they are motivated to make a change through the action of the narrative.
- Central characters will necessarily change slowly during the course of a film.

CHAPTER SIX

TONE

Tone is the overall spirit of a narrative which evokes the passions of its audience and creates a mood. There are infinite ways of manipulating tone. Many are conventions so familiar that they've become cliché. (It seems you can't have a haunted castle without a rain storm and a flash of lightning in the establishing shot.) The concept of tone is abstract, and the process of creating it is where art meets psychology.

When describing the elements of drama, Aristotle referred to the fifth element as "melody." Literally that means the singing (mel) of a narrative (ode). It has also been translated as "music" or "rhythm," but with closer scrutiny, it becomes clear that Aristotle was not merely referring to the music accompanying a play, but the narrative's own inherent melody. He was referring to the overall tone of the narrative.

It is very easy to confuse the elements of tone and presentation. Both elements can be alluded to in a script, but they are ultimately performance based, and for the most part are only manifested in the final film. The distinction between tone and presentation is that tone is subjective whereas presentation is objective. While presentation is about the observable aural and visual elements, tone is about the emotions expressed in a film.

Like a musical melody, tone doesn't exist in any given instant, but rather develops over time.

Most of the earliest efforts in film were devoid of any attempt to create art or to express emotion. Early films lacked tone. They were mere experiments or "actualities" capturing random action, such as people walking in a garden or leaving a factory. They were single shots that lasted only for seconds, so they had virtually no time to develop their own "melody."

Soon, filmmakers turned to gimmicks, spectacles meant only to titillate their audience such as scantily clad dancing girls, an oncoming train, or a bullet headed directly toward the audience. While these gimmicks might have been emotionally evocative to early audiences, they certainly weren't subtle. These films didn't lack tone completely, but early filmmakers lacked the knowledge and tools to express tone well.

Among the earliest innovators of film was a French magician / artist named Georges Méliès. Méliès was known for incorporating elaborately designed sets and props, as well as narrative, into his stage illusions. When motion pictures were invented, he immediately saw the potential and employed the new medium in cinematic illusions for his stage show. As he got more proficient at it, he began creating some of the earliest narrative films, such as his famous *Cendrillon (Cinderella)* (1899), and *Le voyage dans la lune (A Trip to the Moon)* (1902). Méliès' background in art and theatre were instrumental in his turning films into a creative and emotional

Le voyage dans la lune (A Trip to the Moon) (1902)

experience. Many of his films were made in hand-tinted color. From that point forward, tone would be an essential element of film.

In the beginning, film was truly a visual medium. While Thomas Edison made very early attempts to link sight and sound on film, for the most part early films were completely silent. Soon, in an attempt to compete with live theatre, pianists were added in small venues, and musical ensembles were added to larger establishments to supplement the cinema experience. Ultimately the "Mighty Wurlitzer Organ" or even full orchestras would supplement films in large urban movie houses.

By the 1920's, music was an integral part of the movie-going experience, and it remained a standard convention in film even after the emergence of "talkies" in the late 1920's. Today there are two distinct types of sound that combine to relate the narrative and set the tone of a film — diegetic and non-diegetic sound.

Diegesis is a Greek word that means "to narrate." So, diegetic sounds are part of the telling of a story, and non-diegetic sounds are external to the narration.

Diegetic sounds are motivated by the on-screen action. This can include dialogue, background noise, and sound effects related to what is seen on screen. It can also include the environmental sound of things just off screen. For example, traffic noise might be heard outside a window, or a dog could be heard barking off in the distance. Music, when it's motivated by something on screen such an instrument or even a radio, would be considered diegetic.

Non-diegetic sound can move the narrative forward (as in the case of voice-over narration), but more often it is one of the most significant elements in setting the tone of a film. Non-diegetic sound not only includes the film score, but it can also include musical stings and effects used to punctuate scenes. Sometimes characters, places or ideas will have a leitmotif (recurrent musical theme) associated with them such as the famous music accompanying the shark in *Jaws* (1975).

Film establishes tone visually in much the same way that other fine and performing arts do. The director and designers will employ the use of color, line, shape, texture, and space to create the desired tone. Film, however, will go beyond these basic elements and add some that are unique to its medium.

While movement, either actual or implied, is a significant part of other arts, film relies heavily on movement to set the tone. After all, that's why they're called "motion pictures." What's unique to film is that not only do the elements move within the frame (as they would with the performing arts), but the camera (and by extension the spectator) moves as well. This creates a more immersive art, because the audience is integrated into it.

The camera can move in many ways. It can pan across a scene. It can tilt up and down as if the audience were raising or lowering its gaze. It can physically move toward or away from a subject. It can slide side to side. It can crane up in the air or swoop down to the ground. It can follow a moving object. It can glide with smooth precision or wobble to create an unstable effect. It can also accomplish a combination of those things.

Film can also alter its focus in a way that other arts can't. The entire frame could be in focus, creating a very flat image, or a single element might be in focus while the rest of the scene is blurred, creating a sense of depth. The focus can even shift from one element to another in a single shot. An entire scene could be shot with a romantic, slightly blurry focus, or it can be filmed with a very cold sharp focus. It can even be shot using a color filter or be under or overexposed to invoke a mood.

Casino Royale (2006)

The technical aspects of filmmaking such as the camera, type of lens, and film stock can affect the tone of the film as well. The use of a widescreen format and surround sound will certainly affect the mood too. All the design and casting choices, and even an actor's line delivery can affect the tone.

It is important to remember that all the dramatic elements work synergistically. In a successful film, it will be difficult to separate tone from the other elements, because the sum of the other elements creates the tone.

Editing, however, is the most powerful tool for creating tone. There are infinite ways to assemble film footage. The length of a shot, the pace of the edits, the repetition of shots, the juxtaposition of shots, and transitions from one shot to the next (such as fades, jump cuts, wipes, or dissolves) will all greatly affect the tone of the film.

In 1916, Soviet Filmmaker Lev Kuleshov, conducted an experiment to show how editing could affect the tone of a film. He first took footage of a man blankly staring at the camera. The actor, not knowing what the footage would be used for, was expressionless. Then Kuleshov created footage of a bowl of soup, a child in a coffin, and a beautiful woman lying on a divan, and juxtaposed each with the footage of the man. People who saw the film with the soup believed that the man was hungry, those who saw the film with the coffin believed him to be sad, and those who saw the woman believed him to be desirous.

This demonstrates the power of editing and is probably a good indication that editing is more important to communicating a narrative than acting. It's a case of psychological projection. The viewers feel hungry, or sad, or desirous when they see the soup, the coffin, or the

Effekt Kuleshova (1921)

woman, irrespective of the man. However, upon seeing the man, viewers will then project their own feelings back onto the man. This not only demonstrates that audiences share their experiences with the film, but that the tone set by the film can evoke the passion of the viewer.

The visual and aural elements of a film can be assembled in infinite ways to induce the emotions of an audience. Great filmmakers become experts at knowing how to manipulate and meld all the elements to create a tone that will evoke the desired disposition in their audience. However, the context in which a film is viewed, as well as the character, culture, and previous experience of the viewers, coupled with their willingness to suspend their disbelief, will alter how the film is received.

KEY POINTS:

- Tone is the melody of the narrative.
- It evokes the passions of the audience and creates a mood.
- Tone is distinct from presentation in that it's a subjective element.
- Using music to set the tone began in the silent era.
- Both diegetic sound (originating from the world of the film) and non-diegetic sound (external to the world of the film) help to set the tone.
- Visual designers will employ the use of color, line, shape, texture, and space to create the desired tone.
- Film's ability to control the view of the spectator is unique among the arts.
- Movement makes film a more immersive art and allows the filmmaker to have greater control of the tone.
- Tone is manifested by the other elements as well as the filmmakers' technical and artistic choices.
- The use of a widescreen format and surround sound affect the mood too.
- Viewers respond emotionally to the tone of the film first, and then project those feelings back onto the narrative.

- Great filmmakers know how to use tone to create an immersive experience that will move an audience emotionally.

CHAPTER SEVEN

PRESENTATION

The sixth element of drama has been interpreted by theorists in many ways. Aristotle referred to it as *opsis*, the Greek word meaning "vista." In film, it's been interpreted as *mise-en-scène* (French for "staging"). It is all that is seen or heard by the audience. It is ***how*** the other elements are manifested. It is the tangible presentation of the narrative.

It is often stated (somewhat inaccurately) that Aristotle believed this to be the least important narrative element. Aristotle felt it was unnecessary to be concerned with *opsis* because he was addressing playwrights, who had little control over the staging of a play. Indeed, even the modern screenwriter will have less control over this element than the director, designers, and cinematographer. However, some would contend that in film, *opsis* is the most important element of the narrative. Film relies heavily on visual and aural expression. In fact, movie directors are sometimes referred to as *auteurs* (French for authors) because they are the "writers" (creators) of the sensuous aspects of the narrative.

Again, it's easy to confuse the elements of tone and presentation. While tone is about the emotions expressed in a film (via the implementation of the other elements), presentation is about the observable aural and visual elements. Tone is a subjective expression, and *opsis* (presentation) is about the objectively observable elements of film.

Like tone, *opsis* works in a sensuous way. It directly titillates our emotions. Where plot, dialog, character, and theme appeal to us intellectually, tone and *opsis* just ask us to experience the narrative. While the contemplative elements ask you to critique the narrative, tone and *opsis* invite you to suspend your disbelief and experience the narrative.

Some theorists translate *opsis* as "spectacle" instead of "presentation." But, working backward, "spectacle" comes from the Greek word *spectāre*, meaning "to view." Simply put, while *opsis* refers to all that you observe (the presentation), "spectacle" draws your attention to a specific element. Certainly spectacle, as it is typically understood, is the most obvious part of the presentation, but it is only part. Spectacle can be a thing of curiosity (such as an illusion), a thing of contempt (such as violence), a thing of awe (such as a natural wonder), or a thing of admiration (such as a physical feat). Some of the more obvious examples of spectacle in film would be gunfire, explosions, car chases, blood, and graphic sex. But spectacle can be subtler. Profanity, fast editing, brilliant color, extreme close-ups, startles, physical comedy, and even an impassioned kiss might be construed as spectacle. Spectacle is the part of the presentation that demands your attention.

Speed (1994)

When used with restraint, spectacle can be a very powerful tool to punctuate a narrative, but like grammatical punctuation, it can be overdone. An exclamation point can be very effective in writing! But using it in a benign sentence weakens its effectiveness! Ultimately, a greater use of exclamation points has little power at all!!!!!!!!!!!! And when exclamation points completely supplant a sentence's meaning, then . . . !! So it is with spectacle; used with restraint, it can be very effective. However, the overuse of spectacle will flatten a plot because it will no longer build to a climax. Instead the narrative will become all climax, all the time. The abuse of spectacle also supplants the opportunity to develop characters, and obliterates the chance for well-developed dialogue. It can monopolize the tone and minimize theme to the point of insignificance.

This is why people sometimes say, "the book was better." In adapting a book to the silver screen, stories receive not only a new medium, but also, by necessity, a new narrative. The story must be told in a different way. The filmmaker's *opsis* supplants the *opsis* in the reader's mind. A reader will regulate the *opsis* in their mind's eye to be in accord with how they wish to experience the story. A filmmaker, however, will force the *opsis* upon the audience. Texts must necessarily be condensed for film, and given that a picture is worth a thousand words, a filmmaker will rely heavily on images – the presentation – to say more with less.

While spectacle is abundant in contemporary film, it's only fair to point out that film began as pure spectacle. The earliest motion pictures – mere curiosities found in arcades and traveling shows – had virtually no narrative at all. In time, the movies found their narrative voice, but they continued to seek out spectacle such as sound, color, wide screen formats, computer animation, and on and on. Spectacle is addictive; once you experience the high, you become desensitized, and you seek an ever-greater high to stimulate your senses. Now even the most extravagant films won't satisfy contemporary audiences, and they look for spectacle in more immersive experiences in their headphones, on line, and in their gaming systems.

Some will argue that this decadent addiction to spectacle presages the decline of a society. For example, the fall of the Roman empire was preceded by a period

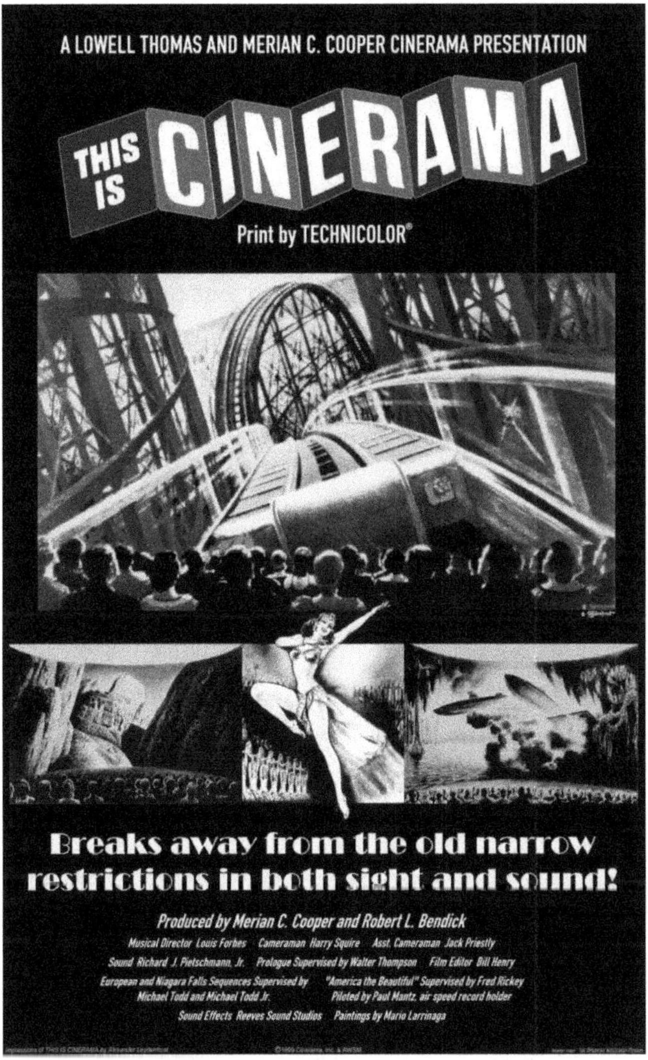

This Is Cinerama (1952)

where the most horrific spectacle of gladiatorial entertainment supplanted more artistic performances.

There is some evidence that watching films with a lot of spectacle, particularly violence, can make an individual who is predisposed to aggression more aggressive. However, the effect on most individuals is negligible. On the other hand, an entire society that indulges in spectacle at the expense of more meaningful art can spiral into a decline. The presentation of spectacle to the masses creates a mob psychology that demands more spectacle. Further, any political attempt to reign in the abuse of spectacle leads to censorship.

Others argue that society doesn't spin further and further into decadence, but experiences a constant pull between a romantic longing for natural simplicity, and a desire for colossal, classically constructed progress. When the film industry was threatened by the introduction of television in the 1950's, motion pictures turned to more bombastic widescreen spectacles to compete. Ultimately this proved unsuccessful, and that period was followed by the embrace of "direct cinema," which sought "truth" through low budget observational documentaries. Today's multimillion-dollar blockbusters compete with the proliferation of low-budget, homemade, internet films, and the back and forth continues.

Budget is the true controlling factor when it comes to *opsis*. The other narrative elements are virtually free. For example, it doesn't really cost more to have great characters or a solid theme, but presentation is directly tied to how much money filmmakers spend. Spending more money doesn't necessarily mean a better presentation though. The optimal production will spend the least amount of money possible to achieve both the desired effect, and a reasonable return on investment.

Cecil B. DeMille was infamous for spending lavish amounts of money on his epics. For *The Ten Commandments* (1923), he built a massive "Egyptian" city in the Guadalupe sand dunes in California. While the film cost $180,000,000, the result was remarkable and it turned a profit. This was not the case with the wasteful *Cutthroat Island* (1995), which cost $98,000,000, but only made $18,300,000. On the other hand, many low-budget B movies such as the marvelous *Cat People* (1942) were amazingly profitable. By keeping much of the action in the shadows to heighten suspense, and borrowing sets previously made for other films, it was completed in just 18 days on a budget of $134,000, but it grossed more than $4,000,000. Still other B movies, such as the infamous *Plan 9 from Outer Space* (1959), came up short by trying to do too much with too little, and the result is laughable. Of course, technological advances permit more to be done with less, and one can only speculate what the famous directors of the past, like the great Orson Welles or the not-so-great Ed Wood, would have been able to accomplish today.

International distribution is another reason more spectacular movies are being released. To reach the largest audience possible, producers create films that

The Ten Commandments (1923)

Plan 9 from Outer Space (1959)

minimize dialogue (which requires subtitles in foreign markets). They also look to make movies that will be accepted across cultural lines. Fantasies, science fiction, films with lots of action, and animated films that can be dubbed in any language are preferred.

If spectacle reaches the point where it overtakes the presentation, it will become the reason to see the film. These films are the "must-see-blockbuster-movie-events-of-the-year" that everyone lines up for, but when the movie-going experience becomes more significant than the story the film is trying to tell, the narrative evaporates. The medium, as Marshall McLuhan observed, truly becomes the message.

KEY POINTS:

- Aristotle referred to the sixth element as *opsis*, a Greek word meaning "vista."
- Others refer to it as *mise-en-scène*, which is French for "staging".
- We refer to it as "presentation" because it should encompass all the things that are seen or heard in a film.
- Aristotle considered presentation (*opsis*) the least of the elements because he was addressing playwrights, who had little control over the staging of a play.

- For filmmakers, presentation is an important element because film relies heavily on visual and aural expression.
- Whereas readers of literature will create the presentation in their mind's eye, filmmakers define the presentation for the viewers.
- Spectacle is the most obvious part of the presentation because it draws attention to itself.
- Spectacle can be a thing of curiosity, contempt, awe, or admiration.
- Spectacle can be a very powerful way to punctuate a narrative, but too much spectacle can overwhelm the narrative.
- While film has always been about spectacle, it is addictive because viewers get desensitized to it, and continually want more.
- While an abundance of spectacle can have a negative psychological impact on some predisposed individuals, it is unlikely that it has a negative impact on society as a whole.
- History shows that society will embrace spectacular presentation and then resist it and then embrace it again in the natural ebb and flow of trends.

Chapter Seven - Presentation

- The quality and content of a film's presentation is directly related to its budget.
- Filmmakers will invest more on a spectacular film because it will have a wider audience both domestically and internationally.

CHAPTER EIGHT

ANALYSIS

As we noted in the introduction, film is more than a coil of celluloid. It's a rhetorical medium, the purpose of which is to convey a message (in the form of a narrative) from the filmmaker to the audience. The film experience only succeeds when the audience receives the message and is moved by it in some fashion. However, often as not, it is the audience that fails the film, and not the film that fails the audience. Viewers frequently fail to reflect on the film they have just watched.

Getting the most out of a film takes a little effort. It doesn't happen automatically. It would be great if appreciating a film were as easy as popping a pill into your mouth or downloading a file into your brain, but it requires effort and contemplation. There are numerous barriers to truly enjoying a film, and many occur before the film even starts.

Begin by asking why you want to watch a film in the first place. Do you want to be informed? Do you want to laugh or cry? Are you looking to share an experience? There are infinite reasons to watch a film but not every film will fill every need.

Blazing Saddles (1974)

Chapter Eight - Analysis

One basic piece of information a moviegoer should know up front is the film's genre. If, for example, a couple wants to share a romantic evening, and they choose to watch Leni Riefenstahl's *Triumph of the Will* (1935), a Nazi propaganda documentary, it's unlikely to satisfy their need. Genres can be hard to pin down because most films are a blend of genres. Generally, if you're interested in seeing a western, you're not in the mood for a comedy, and if you're interested in a comedy, you won't be thinking about westerns. However, there are many comedy westerns such as *Cat Ballou* (1965), *Support Your Local Sheriff!* (1969), *Blazing Saddles* (1974), *Shanghai Noon* (2000), and so on.

So, the first step is to research a film. By knowing who the filmmakers are, who wrote the script, when it was made, how long the film is, etc., filmgoers will have some expectation about what they're going to see, and after the film they'll be able to guage whether the film met their expectations. Fortunately, in the internet age, information is readily available.

Film marketing should be the first place to look for information. Trailers, posters, advertisements, websites, and so forth will tell you what a movie is about, who made it, where and when it's playing, and whether it's garnered any awards or critical acclaim. In general, marketers want to represent their product as earnestly as possible. However, films aren't marketed like most products. Producers are not necessarily interested in repeat business. Because producers are generally keen to get as much money as possible during an opening weekend, they tend to over-hype a bad film before negative word-of-mouth gets around. Before a film is released, it's a good idea to view its marketing with a skeptical eye.

Once a film has been released, reading the reviews and critiques of others can be very helpful, but it's important to consider the source. Some reviewers are more qualified than others. It's great if you have a favorite reviewer who's reliable and shares your sensibilities, but sometimes you might be more interested in knowing what the prevailing public opinion is.

Today, people rely heavily on metadata. They will judge a film based on the average number of "stars" (or other icons) awarded a film by a large number of viewers. These averages can be an accurate and effective way to judge a film, particularly if they're combined with a summary or a review. On the other hand, there can also be a lot of confirmation bias with metadata. These ranking systems can have an over-representation of a self-selected fan base who are predisposed to liking the film. For the most part, only people who are interested in seeing a particular film will watch it and subsequently review it. Even metadata based on the observations of professional critics can be biased.

There is a significant distinction between reviews and critiques. Reviews are very subjective. They're usually just a summary of the narrative, backed up with some casual observations. They read something like this:

"It's a taut drama that will keep you guessing until the very end. I enjoyed the performances and I'm looking forward to the sequel." That's fine if you're chatting with a friend but it lacks authority. Liking or not liking a film is a good start, but being able to explain *why* you did or did not like a film is more insightful and rewarding.

A good critique is more objective than a review. It evaluates the aesthetics of a film and puts it in a meaningful context. There's plenty of room for opinions when critiquing a film, but those opinions must be justified. There are no absolute rights and wrongs when it comes to any art, but there are better and worse choices that can be made.

So, armed with a knowledge of the dramatic elements, you are now ready to begin your own analysis of a film. It takes practice and experience to be a great critic, but anyone can analyze a film. The good news is that your opinion is as valid as anyone else's, and there is a system that can help you analyze a film thoughtfully.

The first step is to approach each film with an open mind and a willingness to suspend your disbelief. This isn't always easy to do. Moviegoers often enter a theater (or approach some other viewing device) with preconceived notions, expectations, or prejudices regarding what they're about to see. That's only natural, but it alters the way a film is perceived. However, these preconceptions can be mitigated by embracing some movie-going rituals. By arriving early, making a routine purchase at the concession stand, having a favorite seat to

111

sit in, and so forth, viewers can put themselves in the neutral frame of mind that allows them to be more objective about what they're going to watch.

Sherlock Jr. (1924)

Remember that "entertainment" is a Latin word that means, "to hold." If a film is doing its job, it will hold your attention throughout. Nonetheless, it is necessary to focus and allow yourself to be drawn into the world of the film. Talking, taking notes, texting on a cellphone, or otherwise diverting your attention from the screen will certainly affect your experience and the subsequent evaluation of the film.

When the closing credits begin to roll, it's time to pause and reflect on your emotions. At this point, "I liked it" or "I didn't like it" are completely valid reactions to the film. While a more intellectual analysis is necessary for a deeper appreciation of a film, the first moments should be reserved for a visceral response.

The next step is to take a preliminary guess as to *why* you did or did not like the film. Usually something will immediately present itself as being the most significant aspect of the film. Of course, it's charitable to consider how the film succeeded before dwelling on its shortcomings. Most films will have some praiseworthy aspect if you consider it long enough.

Remember that there are no right or wrong choices in filmmaking, but there are better and worse choices. It's also a good idea to refrain from second-guessing the filmmakers. How you would have done it differently is irrelevant because it's not your film. A film should be critiqued on its own merits. Consider whether the filmmakers succeeded in creating what they intended. Ultimately your initial feelings (while perfectly valid) should be considered less important than whether the film achieves an aesthetic whole, true to its own principals. For example, even someone who hates science fiction films should be able to evaluate one based on whether it's true to itself and achieves its goal.

Now consider the dramatic elements (plot, theme, character, dialogue, tone, and presentation) one at a time and decide which elements dominate the film. Do all the elements combine to create a satisfying whole?

When examining the plot look at the inciting incident and the climax first. How are those two points

113

related? Does the inciting incident give rise to a dramatic question that's answered by the climax?

If it's difficult to determine what the inciting incident is, look at the climax and work backward. The climax should be found at the end of the movie. Be careful not to confuse the point of profound discovery (anagnorisis) with the climax. Anagnorisis will usually happen at the end of the second act of the three-act structure – about a half hour before the movie ends.

What question is resolved in the climax? If you know that, you will be able to determine when that question was first raised. That will be your inciting incident. Once you know what the inciting incident is, and what the dramatic question and the climax are, the entire plot structure will become obvious.

If the dramatic question is silly or unimportant, it may or may not be an indication of a weak plot. Perhaps the plot is intentionally employing a MacGuffin. In this case, one of the other elements is probably more important. This often happens in comedies, romances, and horror films where a silly plot is practically expected. However, when a plot moves forward in an unmotivated or contrived fashion it weakens the entire film. This is particularly true when a film employs a *Deus ex Machina* to bring the film to its conclusion, or when the film drags on with needless explanation after the climax. Remember: when the monster is dead, the movie is over.

Once you're clear on the dramatic question and the climax, it should be easy to determine the theme. The lesson learned at the point of the climax by the central character (and, by extension, the audience) is the theme. The theme must always take a position. A subject alone is not a theme. A theme must say something about the subject. Even when a film asks viewers to impartially look at all sides of an issue, the film takes a single position; i.e. "people should consider all sides."

While it's likely impossible to create a film with no theme, it is entirely possible to muddle several themes together and create confusion. In fact, many films have left viewers wondering why they spent time watching a pointless contrivance. This can easily happen when writers, actors, directors, producers, and so on, are not working toward a common goal.

Themes should not be confused with genres, styles, conflicts, or motifs. Genre is a system of categorizing films. Style is related to tone, and conflict is part of plot. And while there might be a thematic motif in a film (manifested in the subplots), other elements can form motifs as well. For example, a running joke could be a dialogue motif, or a leitmotif in the musical score would be a tone motif.

Themes can be straightforward or thought-provoking and complex. They can be controversial or universal. It could be instructive to consider whether the filmmakers were trying to persuade the audience or reaffirm their beliefs.

Now consider the characters. Usually, the central character is easily identifiable, but sometimes there is more than one central character. The central character will often be an idea or an object in a documentary, but it will rarely be one in a narrative film. If a narrative film appears to have an idea or an object as the central character, it is more likely a MacGuffin. However, in an allegory, the reverse can be true; the central character could represent an idea.

Consider the trajectory of the central character's fortune. Does his fortune improve or decline? Is he heroic throughout the film or is he a born loser? Analyze this very carefully because it can often be unclear. Central characters will frequently not get the thing they're searching for, but will be better off for having tried. Characters can fail to reach their goal or literally be poorer at the end of the film, but still see their overall fortune rise. Consider *It's a Wonderful Life* (1946). The central character dreams of leaving his small town and adventuring around the world. He fails time after time, but in the end, he learns that ". . . no man is a failure who has friends." (Could that be the theme?) On the other hand, characters can achieve all their desires and find themselves completely dissatisfied. In *Citizen Kane* (1941) the eponymous character is completely successful but ultimately discontented. Once you know the trajectory of the central character, you will know if you are dealing with a rising, fortunate, falling, or unfortunate hero.

Now consider the actors' performances and whether they brought their characters "to life." Sometimes a failure to do so is a failure in casting, but

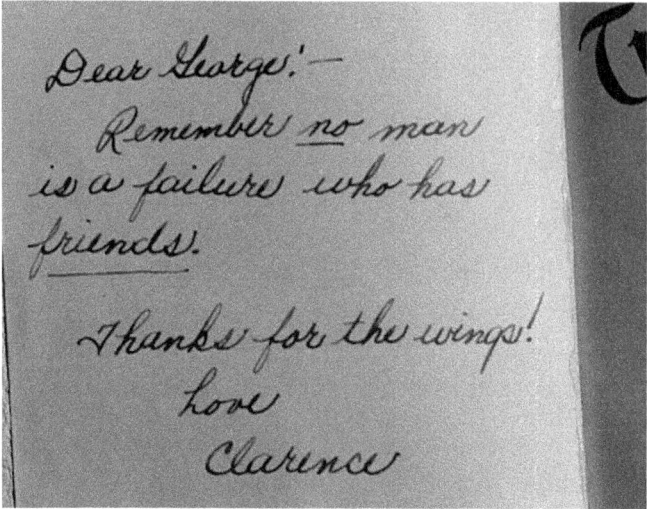

Dear George:—

Remember no man is a failure who has friends.

Thanks for the wings!

Love

Clarence

It's a Wonderful Life (1946)

truly great actors will be able to pull off any role. In fact, casting against type often produces fascinating results and avoids the pitfall of using stereotypes in lieu of archetypes. Consider whether the film used unexpected casting choices to its advantage.

Regardless of casting, a great performance is manifested through an actor's awareness of a scene's conflict. At its heart, a narrative is a series of reactions. Therefore, any given performance will only be as good as the performance of a scene partner. An actor must honestly react to the reactions of the other characters. Further, the central character must be evenly matched with a nemesis. While the central character may have to acquire skills or physical objects that enable him to take on the antagonist, the two characters should be closely matched in the final conflict.

While it's a common belief that an actor's craft is about pretense, a good actor will tell you it's about honesty. When an actor truly understands the character's motivation, the performance will be more honest. If the actor reacts dishonestly, the actor is said to be "out of character." A scene progresses as characters grapple with each other trying to resolve a conflict. Once the conflict is resolved, a new conflict will usually take its place.

Great performances are also tied to the motivation and conflict inherent in the script. If the script lacks conflict, a good actor, director, or editor will often have to compensate with an artificial urgency or conflict. This is particularly true in expository scenes. Early in a film a character often will be preoccupied with daily business (washing dishes, fixing a car, typing, etc.) and an urgency will be manufactured when another character disrupts that business to relay (sometimes banal) information. For example, *The Wizard of Oz* (1939) opens with some farm hands going about their business. Then the central character, Dorothy, interrupts them with what she feels is alarming news about her dog having been mistreated. Conflict arises because it is important to her, but not to anyone else. Nonetheless, the audience learns a great deal of information about the characters who populate the film. The conflict at this point is trivial, but it allows the exposition to be revealed in a motivated fashion.

Another way to examine the use of characters in a film is to consider the presence of archetypes. Does the film put an interesting spin on how it employs the use of familiar archetypes or does the film rely on well-worn, sometimes offensive, stereotypes? Nerds with the bridge of their glasses taped together, women who love to gossip and shop, evil African warlords, giggling prostitutes, homicidal homosexuals, drunken rednecks, and so forth have no depth because they will behave in a fashion that is predictable and will act out with very little motivation. They don't need motivation because the cliché is that they're simply irrational. Shallow films will rely on these caricatures for simplistic laughs or as straw men who can easily be defeated. A better film might toy with these stereotypes, but then give them an interesting twist. For example, Indiana Jones, the central character in *Raiders of the Lost Ark* (1981), appears to be a quiet nerdy archeology professor in his classroom, but outside of the classroom he becomes a rugged, whip-snapping, romantic hero. Somehow, he only needs to wear glasses when he's teaching.

Do you empathize with the central character? Aristotle noted that an audience passes through three stages on the road to empathy: pity, fear, and catharsis. In the first act of a film, you get to know the central character and begin to understand his problems, and consequently pity him. As the second act begins, you fear that he may not succeed. By the climax, you should find yourself emotionally invested in the success or failure of the

119

Raiders of the Lost Ark (1981)

central character. When the central character ultimately does succeed or fail, you should feel a catharsis – a release of your fear. If you fail to pity the central character from the start (perhaps because he's silly or dislikable) or you fail to fear for the central character because he makes unmotivated choices, or the antagonist isn't very threatening, you will ultimately not empathize with the central character and there will be no catharsis at the end.

When considering the dialogue, first decide whether it's honest and appropriate. Did the characters speak only when motivated to do so? Film is a visual medium, which means the dialogue is often minimal and succinct. Films don't usually have time for longwinded discourse. On the other hand, many classic comedies and noir films thrive on witty repartee.

Was the dialogue poetic, crisp, clever, and quotable, or did the director prefer improvised or even mumbled dialogue for a more naturalistic feel? Were there other speech and dialect quirks used to add specificity to the dialogue or to create distinctive characters?

Another function of dialogue is to create conflict. Did the dialogue move the plot forward by creating conflict? Did the dialogue effectively establish the exposition and tie up loose ends after the climax, or did the characters become garrulous, and make the end tedious?

Now consider the final two elements, tone and opsis (or presentation). They're related but distinct. Both are sensuous, experiential elements. They appeal to the viewers' emotions and not their intellect. Presentation encompasses the tangible visual and aural aspects of a film, and tone is the overall feeling expressed across the film. It is the "melody" of the film. To appreciate presentation and tone, consider how the film looked and felt.

Did the tone affect you emotionally? Was it appropriate for the narrative? How did the lighting, color, texture, use of space, rhythm, sound effects, and music affect the tone? How did the editing affect the film? An editor can literally create a visual melody with cuts. Did the tone pull you into the world of the film or did it alienate you?

Next, think about how the film looked and sounded. What was unique about the film's presentation? Was it suited to the narrative? If the narrative was taken from another source, did the film live up to your expectations visually?

Spectacle will be the most obvious part of the presentation and can be a thing of curiosity, contempt, awe, or admiration. What role did spectacle play in the film? Was spectacle used to punctuate the narrative or did it overtake the narrative?

One of the biggest challenges to analyzing a film is committing the time to do it. If a film is two hours long, it can't be watched in one hour. You must commit to the full two hours, but that's not all. If you then want to critique or discuss the film with others, it's going to take even more time. This is why many academic or social screenings of films fall flat. For example, many academic institutions will put together a film festival based on a topic of interest (racism, the environment, politics, etc.) with the intention of having a post-film discussion. The problem is that it requires an interested group to commit to not only the two hours to watch the film, but also enough discussion time for everyone to be heard. If you put together a festival of films that offers varying perspectives, the time requirement is multiplied.

Chapter Eight - Analysis

There are several ways to mitigate this problem. If the head of the festival is prepared with commentary highlighting the most salient issues regarding the films as well some probing questions, the event will run much more efficiently. This will require some preparation and expertise on the part of the leader.

Having a post-film reception will allow attendees to express their views to each other. While this still will require more time, it's more efficient because everyone gets a chance to speak their mind. Further, it will give people a chance to get up and stretch and take a restroom break before the discussion. Further, if cookies and soft drinks (or wine and cheese) are served afterward, audience members will feel more inclined to stay. This works particularly well for film clubs and senior centers.

Another possibility is to provide a website to collect some feedback. Sometimes audience members simply must leave due to other obligations but would still appreciate a way to express themselves. In the case of an issue-oriented film festival this has the added bonus of collecting information about your audience such as contact information. In not-for-profit situations, it might also be a way of collecting donations.

We hope you have found this book instructive. As Socrates said, "The unexamined life is not worth living." We believe that the ability to examine films in a thoughtful way, makes them worth watching. In the appendix of this book you will find a useful list of questions that prompt you to think more deeply about a film. These questions will be particularly useful for engendering conversation in the classroom, at film clubs, and at film festivals.

KEY POINTS:

- To truly appreciate a film, you need to contemplate it.
- Begin by researching a film before watching it.
- Learn about the film through marketing information and reviews.
- Consider the source of reviews and critiques before relying on them.
- Reviews will give an overall impression of a film, but critiques will be more authoritative.
- Metadata reviews can be useful but often have an over-representation of a self-selected fan base.
- Moviegoers should approach a film with a willingness to suspend their disbelief.
- Engaging in a pre-film ritual will help put you, the viewer, in a neutral disposition.
- It is important to give the film your full attention.
- When the film has finished, take a moment to consider your overall impression of the film.

- Be charitable and look for the positive qualities of the film first.
- Refrain from second-guessing the filmmakers.
- A film should be critiqued on whether the film achieves an aesthetic whole, true to its own principals.
- Consider each of the dramatic elements and decide which elements dominate, and if the elements are blended well.
- Look for the key plot points and the dramatic question.
- Consider what the theme of the film is.
- If the theme is repeated in subplots, it might be a thematic motif.
- Consider whether the filmmakers were trying to persuade the audience or reaffirm their beliefs.
- Decide who the central character is, and the trajectory of his fortunes.
- Casting an actor against "type" can avoid stereotypes even while embracing archetypes.
- Great films will use genuine motivation and conflict to move the plot forward.
- A good film will make use of Aristotle's pity, fear, and catharsis model.
- Dialogue will usually be honest, appropriate, minimal, and succinct

125

- Some films will rely on witty banter for effect.
- Dialogue can move a plot forward by creating conflict.
- Some films use improvised dialogue, or speech and dialect quirks to create distinctive characters.
- Dialogue will also establish the exposition and tie up loose ends after the climax.
- Tone and opsis (presentation) are sensuous elements.
- Tone is the "melody" of the film.
- Presentation encompasses the tangible visual and aural aspects of a film.
- Tone and presentation can pull you, the viewer, into the world of the film or it can alienate you.
- Spectacle can be a thing of curiosity, contempt, awe, or admiration.
- Spectacle should punctuate the narrative but not overtake it.
- Analyzing a film requires a time commitment.
- That time commitment can be a challenge for academic film festivals, or film clubs.

- This can be mitigated somewhat by having prepared remarks and questions.
- A post-film reception will allow time for attendees to express their views.
- It might also be useful to provide a website to collect feedback and contact information.

APPENDIX

The questions provided here are meant as a guide for those critiquing a film, introducing a film to an audience, writing an academic paper, or trying to engender conversation in a group setting. Of course, these questions are also great for self-reflection and post-film conversations with friends.

Obviously, not all these questions will be pertinent to all films, but most will apply to most films. It should also be noted that these questions are focused on narrative films. While most documentaries will follow a narrative structure (making many of these questions valid), narrative films have additional attributes which will be addressed in volume two of the handbook.

Take your time answering these questions. The answers may seem obvious at first, but upon further reflection or investigation even the most straightforward questions might surprise you. For example, the question of who directed a film seems simple enough, but sometimes a film will have more than one director or the identity of the director will be in doubt. For *Poltergeist* (1982), Tobe Hooper, best known as the creator of *The Texas Chainsaw Massacre* (1974), is the director of record, but those who worked on the film say that the movie's writer, Steven Spielberg, was actually at the helm of the film. Spielberg has denied this, but members of the cast and crew stand by it. Spielberg and Hooper have very different styles and reputations, so it is instructive to examine the film in that light.

Steven Spielberg, Tobe Hooper, James Karen and
Craig T. Nelson on the set of *Poltergeist* (1982)

Examining films using these questions might seem laborious at first, but in time narrative analysis will become second nature. Film appreciation is not about having an encyclopedic knowledge of film history; there are reference books and the internet for that. The goal is simply to understand *why* you did or did not appreciate a certain film. When you can do that, you will be a true film fanatic.

BEFORE THE FILM

- Why are you watching this film?
- What is the film's genre?
- When was the film made?
- Who is the producer?
- Who is the writer?
- Who is the director?
- Who are the main actors?
- Are there other noteworthy artists associated with the film?
- What other films have the producer, writer, director, etc. made?
- What is your impression of those other films?
- Is the film derived from another source such a book?
- What do you know about the other source?
- What have others said about the film?
- What did the critics and reviewers say about the film?
- How have other viewers reacted to the film?
- How good are the metadata ratings (star ratings) for the film?
- What is the MPAA rating for the film?

- What do the parental guides say about the film?
- What are your expectations the film?

DURING THE FILM

- Were there distractions during the film such as cell phones or talking?
- Were you able to focus on the film or was your mind elsewhere?
- Where did you watch the film?
- Were you able to suspend your disbelief?
- Did you see this film by choice or did someone persuade you to see it?
- Did you react emotionally to the film (laugh, cry, etc.)?
- How did others in the audience react?

AFTER THE FILM

- What was your first impression when the film ended?
- Did the film "entertain" you (hold your attention)?
- What is your favorite thing about the film?

- Are there obvious weaknesses with the film?

- Does the film have a good title?

- Does the film achieve its own aesthetic goals?

- Did the filmmakers accomplish what they intended?

- Are the dramatic elements blended together well?

- Which dramatic element takes precedence?

- How will the film play for varying cultures and foreign markets?

- Who is the target audience for the film?

PLOT

- Does the fortune of the central character rise, remain fortunate, fall, or remain unfortunate?

- What is the point of attack (the very first moment) in for the film?

- Does the film begin *in medias res* (in the middle of things)?

- Describe the primary stasis (ordinary life) at the beginning of the film.

- How is the exposition laid out?

- Is there sufficient exposition before the inciting incident?
- What is the inciting incident?
- How quickly does the action rise?
- What is the central question?
- Is there a point of anagnorisis – a moment of profound discovery – in the film?
- Is there peripeteia – a sudden reversal – in the film?
- What is the climax – point of maximum tension – of the film?
- Is the central question answered in the climax?
- Describe the secondary stasis.
- How are things different at the end of the film relative to the beginning?
- Does the film end shortly after the climax or does it continue needlessly?
- Does the film use a *deus ex machina* – an unexpected power or event saving a seemingly hopeless situation – to resolve the narrative?
- Does the film presage a sequel by introducing a new central question?

- Does the film use a MacGuffin – a thing of no consequence– to drive the story forward?
- Does the film have a clear three-act structure?
- Does the inciting incident come ¼ of the way into the film?
- Does anagnorisis come ¾ of the way into the film?

DIALOGUE

- Does the film rely on dialogue to tell the story more, or less than the visuals?
- Is the amount of dialogue appropriate for the narrative?
- Is the dialogue honest and motivated relative to the world of the film?
- Is the dialogue differentiated between characters or do they all speak the same?
- Does the film employ longwinded speeches or is the dialogue short and pithy?
- Does the film use subtext effectively or does it devolve into sarcasm?
- Is the expository dialogue honestly motivated?

- Does the film use dialogue for long post-climax explanations?
- Is the dialogue elevated and poetic or prosaic and base?
- Does the dialogue seem improvised?
- Is the dialogue mumbled or otherwise difficult to understand?
- Does the improvised dialogue seem realistic or tortuous?
- Are title cards or a narrator used in lieu of dialogue?

THEME

- What is the theme of the film?
- Is the theme in harmony with the other elements?
- Does the theme take a clear position, or does it merely consider an issue?
- Does the theme form a motif throughout the film?
- Is the theme muddled with other sub themes?
- Is the theme significant or inconsequential?

- Does the film make a political or social statement?
- Is the theme empowering or cynical?

CHARACTER

- Who is the protagonist?
- Who is the antagonist?
- How do the protagonist and antagonist change over the course of the film?
- Are the protagonist and antagonist evenly matched?
- Which characters align themselves with the protagonist?
- Which characters align themselves with the antagonist?
- Are there any contagonists – well-meaning characters who obstruct things – in the film?
- Did you pity and fear for the central character?
- Is the protagonist a rising, fortunate, falling, or unfortunate hero?
- Is the protagonist a reluctant hero?
- Is the protagonist an antihero?
- Does the central character suffer from hubris?

- Are there more than one central character?
- Is the protagonist an allegorical figure?
- Are the characters presented as archetypes or stereotypes?
- Were the characters immediately identifiable as certain archetypes?
- How do the characters in this film compare to similar archetypes in other films?
- Were there any "everyman" characters in the film?

TONE

- What is the overall mood of the film?
- Were you sucked into the world of the film emotionally, or were you a dispassionate viewer of the film?
- How did your own mood and willingness to suspend your disbelief affect the emotional experience of watching the film?
- How does the cinematography affect the tone?
- How does the editing effect the mood of the film?
- Does the film use a hard or soft focus?

- Does the film progress smoothly from scene to scene or are the transitions jarring?
- Does the musical score set and support the tone of the film?
- Are there any leitmotifs used in the film?
- Is surround sound used to affect the mood?
- How do the actors' performances contribute to the tone of the film?
- Is film in black and white or color?
- How vibrant is the color and how did that affect the mood?
- Does the screen size affect the mood?
- How are the visual elements of color, line, shape, texture, space, and light used to create the desired mood?

PRESENTATION

- How does the film look?
- Are the design elements (makeup, costumes, props and sets) appropriate and effective?
- Is the director's staging – *mise-en-scène* – effective?

- If the film is derived from another source, such as a book, how does it compare to your expectations visually?

- Are elements of spectacle (curiosity, contempt, awe, or admiration) present in the film?

- Are computer-generated images a noticeable part of the film?

- Are the computer-generated images effective or distracting?

- Does the spectacle punctuate the narrative or overwhelm it?

- Do you have a predisposition to like or dislike an abundance of spectacle?

- Did the size of the film's budget affect its presentation?